"*Carnival of the Spirit* allows the reader to tap into the magic that occurs when we are grateful for life's holiness, showing us ancient ritual ways to celebrate our humanness. I loved it!"

Jamie Sams
author of *Earth Medicine*

"Luisah Teish is a gifted teller of tales and myth. She has the ability to transcend time, and differences of culture and environment, with rites and rituals to reconnect us with our spiritual origins here and now. We thoroughly enjoyed this book!"

Pauline and Dan Campanelli
authors of *Wheel of the Year* and *Ancient Ways*

"Osun's child, Luisah Teish, has called a meeting of woman force. In these pages, the daughters of the sun romp with their moon sisters, the tide maidens soothe the earth mother, and the wild women of the whirlwind shoot sparks to light the universe. Read, savor, learn, and be healed. Adupe Luisah."

Jessica Harris
author of *Natural Beauty from the Majority World*

⁓· *Carnival of the Spirit* ·⁓

✦· *Carnival* ·✦
of the
Spirit

*Seasonal Celebrations and
Rites of Passage*

Luisah Teish

HarperSanFrancisco
A Division of HarperCollinsPublishers

CARNIVAL OF THE SPIRIT: *Seasonal Celebrations and Rites of Passage.* Copyright ©
1994 by Luisah Teish. All rights reserved. Printed in the United States of America.
No part of this book may be used or reproduced in any manner whatsoever without
written permission except in the case of brief quotations embodied in critical articles and reviews. For information address HarperCollins Publishers, 10 East 53rd
Street, New York, NY 10022.

Illustrations by Luisah Teish, David Wilson, Kim Green, and Teresa Roberts.

FIRST EDITION

Library of Congress Cataloging-in-Publication Data
Teish, Luisah.
    Carnival of the spirit : seasonal celebrations and rites of
passage / Luisah Teish. — 1st ed.
        p.   cm.
    ISBN 0–06–250868–7
    1. Religious calendars.   2. Rites and ceremonies.
    3. Seasons—Religious aspects.   4. Yoruba (African people)—
    Religion—Miscellanea.   I. Title.
    Bl590.T45   1994
    299'.64—dc20   90–55784
                                                           CIP

    94   95   96   97   98   ❖   HAD   10   9   8   7   6   5   4   3   2   1

This book is dedicated to
Oshun Olo'shogbo, Goddess of the River,
to the ancestor Ethel Waters,
and to Mermaids everywhere.

Contents

Acknowledgments ix

Preface xi

Introduction 1

Creation 11

Winter
Mother of the Night

21

Spring
The Daughter of Promise

73

Summer
The Bride of Summer

121

Autumn
Lady of the Sunset

159

Notes 221

Index 225

Acknowledgments

Praise and Love to those who seek, to those who know, and those who speak:

Praise and Love to Babalawo Bolu Fatunmise of Ile Ife, Nigeria, for kinship and for my chieftancy title.

Praise and Love to Iyalode Oshun of Oshogbo, Nigeria, for feeding my tongue.

Praise and Love to Babalawo Adesanya of Ode Remo, Nigeria, for confirming my destiny.

Praise and Love to Iyare Olokun of Benin City, Nigeria, for teaching me how to swallow the Moon.

Praise and Love to Babalawo Medahoche and Iya Alase Noche of Milwaukee, Wisconsin, for my rebirth ritual.

Praise and Love to Iya l'orisha Omi Aladora of Miami Beach, Florida, for helping me to crack the ancestral code.

Praise and Love to the members of Ile Orunmila Oshun and Ile Alaketu 'ti Oshun of Oakland, California, for faith, encouragement, and support.

Praise and Love to the ancestors of Goree Island and the Middle Passage for mighty shoulders to stand on.

To the staff of Harper San Francisco, to Jacque and Janine Vallee, Nzinga Denny, Kim Green, and Jodi Sager of the Bay Area; to William and the Amsterdam group, to my sisters in Australia and New Zealand, to the Arcania clan in Bath, England, to the Sinhas in Bahia, Brazil. To all the librarians, the storytellers, and the MacIntosh girls. To all the patient people who lit orange candles and chanted the mantra "finish the book and go to bed," I say Praise, Praise and Love to all my relations.

Preface

Each year millions of people walk outside their shelters, look at the sky, smell the wind, and make plans for the coming seasons.

Many of these people will repeat the physical and ceremonial acts prescribed by their culture and religion for centuries. Some will want to honor the ways of the past but need something more personal, more directly related to their own experience and desires. Others will find that they have needs for which no ritual currently exists. This book is written for the creative person who seeks to honor the past in a new way.

Carnival of the Spirit integrates the ritual and ceremonial practices of several "tribal peoples" with the perceived needs and demands of our times. This blend of practices is flavored by the influence of Yemonja and Oshun.

Yemonja is the Mother Goddess, whose power is manifested in family life and domestic affairs. She nurtures us through the cycles of Life. She teaches us to walk and talk, from infancy to maturity.

Oshun, the Yoruba Goddess of Love, Art, and Sensuality, represents the Erotic in Nature. She also brings culture and refinement to human life. Through Her, walking evolves into Dance, talking becomes Song.

When Yemonja and Oshun flow together, everyday life becomes a celebration. I am Their servant, Their taste-tester, Their transcriber.

Although much of this book is drawn from Yoruba culture, it is not a book of orthodox Yoruba ritual. Neither is it a book about Santeria—an Afro-Cuban cult recently (circa 1940) immigrated to the United States. This is a book about the seasons of the Earth and the effect they have had on individual and community life for thousands of years. Spring. Summer. Fall and Winter. Virtually all people on Earth celebrate the passage of time with food, music, dance, offering, and the reenactment of myth. Everywhere a harvest is celebrated.

This book is transcultural. It discusses the cultural notations that have been made on eco-centric reality. The eco-centric reality, the nature of the land a people inhabit, contributes more to ceremonial similarities and differences than skin color, hair texture, or buttock size.

The Transcultural Past

Centuries ago the trans-Atlantic slave trade brought millions of Black people from their motherland, Africa, to the so-called New World. They were dispersed throughout the Western Hemisphere, with large concentrations in Brazil, the Caribbean Islands, and the North American colonies. In those places, Native American folk-knowledge, pagan ceremonial practices, and enforced Christian theology were added to their own beliefs and practices.

The Catholic church sponsored the slave trade and demanded that their critters be baptized, take Christian names, and worship the saints. In most places the Black Codes forbade slaves to marry, own property, speak their own language, or worship their gods.

But like most people, the Africans managed to acclimate themselves to the land, people, and culture around them. And in the process they created rituals and celebrations that are both old and new. This is true everywhere that people of African descent are found.

My own quest for spiritual liberation began with Egypt, the wonderful, mystical cradle of civilization. The quest for Cosmic Joy took me to Africa where the deities walk among human beings and dance *is* worship. The need to walk in balance was answered by my Native American ancestors. The culture's call to Earth reverence and stewardship resonates with Ibo theology (Nigeria) and is imperative to health in this time of ecological crisis. The African and Native American traditions are blessed with elders who have preserved the stories and rituals in spite of centuries of oppression.

So the ceremonial practices examined here are primarily African. But Native American and pre-Christian European practices are also considered because they have contributed to the diaspora. Eastern and South Pacific cultures are given honorable mention where appropriate. Everywhere the Earth is revered.

Somewhere in the distant past our ancestors observed certain truths about the activities of Nature and the behavior of human beings. Whether it was done intuitively or scientifically, they created songs, dances, and rituals with the intention of recognizing, attuning with, and celebrating the seasons. Tradition was based on the needs of the time and on the perceived needs of the future. Today we must access the needs of our time and determine *what* should be done differently. If we are wise, what we create will take us into the future. To create wisely we must understand the thoughts and feelings that led our ancestors to action.

This book will explain the origin of well-known holidays and introduce some that are unknown in the Western world. It follows the Western Sun-oriented calendar.

My intent in writing this book is to invite you to a closer alignment with your environment and to promote extended family unity. The book contains guidelines and suggestions for creating your own celebrations. Examples of rituals performed by my extended family are given. I hope they inspire you to creativity and beauty.

Folk and Family Lore

As a storyteller I experience myth and folklore as one of the great ancestral gifts. They tell us what a people think of themselves and their world. The origins of most beliefs and practices can be found in those stories. *Carnival of the Spirit* is laced and embroidered with myth, folklore, and poetry.

Three kinds of tales are presented here: authentic, composite, and original.

The Authentic Tales: The authentic tales are the product of a tribe of people. They belong to no individual but come from ancestral memory. I have treated them in two ways: repeated and returned.

A repeated tale is simply that. It is repeated directly as told to me by elders or quoted from an anthology.

A returned tale is one whose message is essentially the same as it has been for centuries, but I have adjusted the environment and updated the language to clarify its relevance to our times. I have taken the old message and turned it into the morning news.

The Composite Tales: At times I weave together a collage of tales from several cultures. This is done to show the compatibility and continuity of the tale and to compensate for what has been lost through cultural rape. Folktales and folk customs have always borrowed from each other to create an understanding of our collective experience.

I don't, however, say that a tale is African if my source is Native American. That is cultural rip-off. If it is a "Southern tale" with African people on a Native American landscape, both of these factors are acknowledged. Sometimes I combine a returned tale with modern information to illustrate their shared wisdom.

The Original Tales: The original tales are personal. They are dramatizations of episodes from my own life. Some also describe the experiences of extended family members, workshop participants, and ritual attenders. I record their experiences with their permission. In instances where I *must* camouflage certain facts I have used a label name (Sister A), changed the date (once upon a time), or renamed the city (Yuppieville). This is to protect the privacy of those involved. The sequence of events, the emotional reactions, and the consequences of the ritual remain accurate. Stories from my personal experiences are presented with all the understanding and humor that *hindsight* bestows. In all cases the sources are cited and credit is given where credit is due.

If you record your experiences with seasonal rituals, eventually your family will produce a body of folklore about itself. These stories yield insight and are a lot of fun.

Happy Holidays

There are as many seasonal celebrations as there are days of the year. Time and space require that I make some choices and assumptions.

This book assumes that you live in a community of women, men, and children; and that you love and respect Nature. It assumes you have a need and a desire to create rituals. I have chosen to discuss specific culturally based holidays (Christmas, Día de los Muertos, Yam Festival) in the narrative. But my ritual recommendations are "generic." They address the characteristics of the season (Winter) belonging to all who experience it. They are recommendations, not dictates. Use them as guidelines for creating your own rituals. Tailor them to suit your own needs and circumstances.

Most of the rituals require a small budget and a lot of creative work. You may increase the budget, but the beauty and power of the ritual will be lost if you decrease the creative work. You may perform these rituals in conjunction with or instead of the conventional holidays. Minimally, the seasonal celebration should occur in its season. Dress for the weather!

This book is written to help you celebrate life: to enliven your spirit, to stimulate your mind, to beautify your body, and to strengthen the bonds of your community.

It is a gift from the Goddesses, from Yemonja and Oshun. It is written in Their voice, Their tone. I have put pen to paper and transcribed Their song.

May the music of the Mother and the Muse dance through your life and that of the planet eternally. To all my relations, give thanks for life.

In Kinship

Yeye'woro Luisah Teish

TheaScribe

Introduction

The Old Folks Say

What's yo' name now chile?
Whitley did you say?
Are you any kin to . . . ?
Did yo' people come from
down round Texas way?

Say yo' grandpa worked the railroad?
How they call his name?
Was he a tall man with big eyes?
Was his wife called . . . Auntie Mame?

Did yo' grandma have 'leven chillun?
Nine boys and two gals with buck teeth.
Was yo' Uncle Joe a cattle man
Or did Joe herd up sheep?

You sho walk a lot like my sister
Hips justa swaying to & fro.
Girl ya might be my second cousin
With colored folk, ya just never know.

Well they busted up our families.
And they sold the chillun apart.
We ain't got no papers for knowing
Just a funny kind of thump in de heart.

Guess the name don't matter none
Whitley, Jackson or Mo'
If the skin is black and the eyes shiny.
Then we be kinfolk for sho.

Luisah Teish, 1984

Food and Spirits

As a child I enjoyed the fuss and fanfare of the holidays. In my mother's household Thanksgiving and Christmas were always big affairs, especially in the kitchen.

We never made a lot of fuss over the Christmas tree or the Easter baskets. The dinner table and the food were the main attractions. We took a fold-up table out of the closet and pushed it flush with the kitchen table. The table was set with a linen cloth, blue pattern plates, silverware, the "good" glasses (which came in a box of oatmeal), and a bottle of Manischewitz or Mogen David wine. My mother never allowed any other wine on the table. She said it was "holy" wine. As a child I knew nothing about kosher products and still do not know how we came to respect a Jewish tradition in a Black Catholic household.

On holidays our kitchen and living room became "the front room," where eating, dancing, singing, and general socializing took place. The "back room" (the bedrooms) became the nursery and

dorm for children and elders to lie down, and the bathroom remained itself. The house was magically transformed with pieces of
cloth, lamp shades, and bowls of fruit and nuts laid about.

But the real magic was the cooking. It took several days to prepare all the food. Let's say the turkey got thawed on Wednesday af-
ternoon. We didn't just throw it in a pan of water and let it ride.
Oh no! We had a ritual: Take the turkey and set it in the sink with
the plastic wrapper in place. When the ice begins to melt on the
outside of the package, take the plastic off and place the turkey in a
pan with slightly warm water (never hot!). As the turkey thaws,
this water gets cold and has to be replaced.

Eventually the turkey would yield its inner bag, and the neck,
liver, and gizzard were removed. The neck was then thrown in a
pot to boil until the meat fell off the bone. This meat was minced
and put aside in a bowl. Later it would be stirred into a brown
gravy made of turkey stock and flour.

A big pan of cornbread was made, unleavened but with lots of
butter. It would be set aside while my sisters and I chopped seasoning for the dressing: yellow and green onions, celery, garlic, and
bell peppers. Moma would sprinkle black pepper and seasoning
salt with minced garlic on the inside and outside of the turkey.
Then we'd put the unbaked turkey in the refrigerator for a few
hours to "let the seasoning settle in." We referred to him as "Mr.
Turkey" and told him how good he would look and taste.

The unleavened cornbread and chopped seasoning would be
mixed together with oysters, shrimp, or sausage, moistened with
turkey stock, and sprinkled with sage. Voilà! This was homemade
dressing. The turkey would be stuffed in its belly and neck cavity,
dripped with a seasoned butter, and covered with a wet tea towel.

3

The pot was covered and placed in a slow oven so that the turkey cooked overnight. Several times this pot would be opened to the sound of oohs and aahs and the smell of wonder.

This journey into the world of holiday cooking began on Thanksgiving with the turkey and ended on New Year's with Creole cabbage. Holiday cooking usually took about three days. What a ritual it was! There was the business of how fine or how coarse to chop this or that vegetable. We watched yeast dough rise and get punched down again. At some point Aunt Marybelle Reed (Ibae)* or Miz Theresa would come by to debate the virtues of butter versus oleo or try their best to get my mother to accept an iceberg lettuce salad. But Moma would have none of it. A large pot of hot eggnog was made and neighbors dropped by to get a glass (with brandy or rum), report their cooking progress, fuss about something in the news, or recount stories that had changed some small but significant thing about their lives. Take lettuce salad for example:

> *Way back in nineteen forty-ought something, Miss Irene went into a restaurant in downtown New Orleans. It was one of them semichic places down on Canal Street not too far from the ferry. It was one of the few nice places where colored people could eat downtown. Miss Irene went in and ordered crab cakes and lyonnaise potatoes and of course a salad came with it. The waitress took her order cheerfully and returned in a few minutes with a bowl of salad and a Barq's root beer. The salad had several kinds of lettuce in it, along with some green onions, mushrooms, and pieces of bright red tomatoes. Miss Irene had asked for Thousand Island*

---

* Ibae: a salutation of blessing for those who have passed over.

dressing on the side. As she began to toss her salad (a prelude to adding the dressing), she looked down into that bowl and saw something moving. She tilted the bowl in the direction of the sunlight and beheld a worm wiggling 'round on a leaf of iceberg lettuce. Miss Irene was appalled by this sight and called the waitress to the table. "Look, there's a worm rolling around in my salad," she complained excitedly. The waitress picked up a fork, sorted through the salad, and located the worm wedged between a lettuce leaf and a slice of mushroom. The waitress calmly removed the worm. "This happens all the time," she said. "The iceberg lettuce worm is not dark green or brown; it's the same pale green as the lettuce. So they get overlooked in the washing." The waitress smiled. Well, Miss Irene declared that she would just leave that lettuce alone since she preferred not to eat worms at all. So from that day forward Miss Irene stopped eating green salad in public places. Tomatoes, cucumbers, macaroni or potato salad were fine, but not green salads in public places. Further, iceberg lettuce was forever banned from the kitchen of Miss Irene. And to this day she and her children boycott iceberg lettuce for personal as well as political reasons.

Mushrooms were another thing we just didn't bother with. They were toadstools—devil's bread—and we really couldn't understand why fancy folks on TV made such a fuss over them.

Clean and tasty food was more important than fancy toys. We children knew that the packages under the Christmas tree would be clothes, housewares, and school supplies. Perhaps children then were not subject to the hard-sell approach that today's youngsters face. But in low-income families clothes were the good gift. In fact,

I remember a year when a local Catholic group gave toys away. Each child walked down a long assembly line of things and was allowed to choose one item. I selected a hoola hoop and my friends made it clear that they thought it was a silly choice. I should have gotten a doll with clothes.

My dolls were handmade, simple—a soft drink bottle with hair made from dried Spanish moss. The hair was secured with a wooden clothespin. We could braid and decorate this hair all day, wrap skirts and shawls around the dolls, and change their names simply by changing the hair from moss to rope.

I remember the food and the socializing as the great things about the holidays. Seeing Aunt So-and-So and tasting her all-butter pound cake. Smelling the cigar smoke in the next room where the uncles exaggerated their exploits and the aunts laughed about how fast the children were growing and what a cute thing Johnny Jr. did the other day. Holding the new baby and feeling the soft warmth of her touch. Being inside where it was warm with food and friends.

The holidays were also a time to extend yourself to those who were less fortunate because we did, after all, have food, shelter, and each other. So we looked in on the old folks, and forgave the people who'd offended us, and resolved that something was going to be different somehow. Somewhere in this agenda church fit in: a midnight mass, a sunrise service, listening to the choir wail, and watching the appropriate Bible movie on television.

For me it was midnight mass on Christmas Eve and sunrise service at Easter. Miz Theresa was my church buddy. She was the wife of a member of my mother's extended family. Her husband's grandmother was the midwife who'd delivered my mother. Moma had been his baby-sitter as a teenager and now I was assistant cook and bottle-washer for his wife. Miz T. held a special place in our extended family. She was a cross between auntie and friend. She was not kin by blood but by loyalty and spirit. She was almost a godmother, kinda like a cousin, definitely a good neighbor. She paid me to do what I would have done freely. The work done at her house was really supplementary instruction to the training I received at home. I learned how to make a bed properly, count money, comb my hair.

People such as this were called Auntie and Uncle, Moma Blue and Poppa Black, Miz T. and Cousin B. They often discussed with you the things your parents were too embarrassed to talk about—like sex and race relations; and they spoke to your parents on your behalf, increasing your freedom, offering another point of view, respectfully. I am grateful to have had such people in my life.

Well, Miz T. and I went to the Catholic church together. We would dress up in ruffled dresses on Christmas Eve and wide-brimmed hats adorned with flowers on Easter. We'd get in her car and drive to All Saints Church for mass.

Supposedly, at midnight on Christmas Eve all the cows, goats, and horses would lower their heads and say a prayer (for one full minute) in honor of the Christ child. I was never able to test this myth as a youngster because I was always in bed waiting for Santa or at church with my own head bowed.

Every Easter my mother would remind us that "even if Christ did come back, these fools would kill him the first time he opened his mouth."

Halloween, Thanksgiving, Christmas, New Year's, Mardi Gras, Easter, and the Fourth of July—the holidays were regarded, in general, as a time to exhibit different behavior and to enjoy oneself.

When I grew older and left home, I was thrown into circles of people who treated the holidays differently. There was less emphasis on food and clothes, more emphasis on money and things. Being at home together was not as important as being in the "right" place, being seen with the "cool people." This is called adolescence (no matter at what age it occurs).

As adolescence stretched out into young adulthood I watched the holidays become a time of false piety, social snobbery, and conspicuous consumption.

By the time I reached college I'd taken a political position against the holidays—period. They were just another excuse to beat people out of their money, lay somebody off a job, tell another lie about the past, bow down to a white baby boy, look up to a bleeding statue, or act out strange behaviors without understanding what they meant.

This was followed by my "Black pride and awareness" period. To give meaning to an otherwise meaningless year, I turned everything Black. Jesus, Mary, and Joseph became Black. That winter holiday was now spelled Xmas for the unknown truth, and Easter became Black. New Year's remained nebulous while Thanksgiving became the "Criminals' Holiday" on which I railed against exploitation of Native Americans.

In the late sixties (which were really the early seventies) I joined the Fahamme Temple of Amun-Ra in St. Louis. Here I learned Egyptian beliefs about the solstices and equinoxes, was taught to analyze the symbols associated with holidays, and was made to understand that the daily rising and setting of the Sun make each day a "holy day." I felt a little better.

When I moved to the San Francisco Bay Area (circa 1971) I participated in Kwanzaa celebrations. Somehow I fell naturally into the role of "name composer." People who wanted to change their names at this ceremony consulted with me for suitable African names. That felt really good.

Somewhere along the line I decided that I would celebrate the birthdays of my friends (but not my own), Mother's Day, Juneteenth, International Women's Day, and a personal holiday I created for myself called The Reformation. Thanksgiving was reclaimed in my world as Indian Harvest. Living with people from Latin cultures taught me to love and respect Día de los Muertos. My Wiccan sister, Starhawk, threw some light on Halloween and suddenly the day made sense.

As I grew older, I met many people from diverse cultures and began to share in their celebrations with them.

Today I celebrate the seasons with rituals from all over the world. Occasionally I am fortunate enough to participate in large public rituals on ancient "sacred sites." Most often, however, my seasonal celebrations are held at my home with extended family members. And a few of the rituals are based on the astrological aspects of the day/hour. These are simple, personal, and secret.

I have learned that every day is a Holy Day. And the Earth is a sacred place where the power of the Sea and the beauty of the Sky express Mother Nature's love for humanity, and the wonder of Creation.

Creation

In the beginning, at a time when there was no Time, all that existed was the great silence in the dark depth of the Cosmic Womb (Nana Buluku). Within the Womb the Great Egg of the World (Olodumare) sat in patient potential waiting for the fated moment of its hatching. Suddenly a sound burst out from the center of the egg—OOORRRROOO—and the life-giving particles in the egg quickened and set into motion a tremendous bang (Okanran), causing creative air spirits (Eleda) in the form of gases to dance among themselves.

They danced themselves into Fire; they danced themselves into Earth. In the frenzy of their joy, Moon (Mawu) and Sun (Lisa) were born.

Other dancing gases clashed and collided into fireballs spinning through the deep blue of space. They leaped and tumbled into the luminous depth of the Earth and formed the Ocean (Yemaya-Olokun). The rushing hum of the Ocean splashed Itself against Earth's shores, as the great masses of land erupted from Her depth (Ile).

Sun stepped forward to perform His solo and the Moon laid back to cool Herself off in the Upper Deep. As the Sun performed His slow drag over the surface of the Earth, life stirred in His rays (Ache). In the depth of the Sea things began to form—a single cell divided into two making seaweed, hydra, and fish. The crab crawled out of the water and found that on the land life was moving; seed burst open forming flowers, trees, and fruit. Spiders crawled, birds flew, and bush cows roamed in the forest. A blazing heat permeated the Earth, causing all things to stir and take shape. But His heat was overwhelming, things were being overdone, so He receded and the Moon brought forth Her dance. She circled slowly through the night sky cooling the Earth, settling seed, calming the waters, and leaking a mysterious ray of subtle light (Ache) that tempered everything on Earth.

The Moon called out, alarmed by the magnitude of the work they had done. Her cry resounded to the depths of the Earth, and up from the center came the Rainbow Serpent (Damballah Hwedo). The Serpent wrapped Itself around the Earth and the Sky, holding the two together like a covered calabash.

Sun and Moon smiled at the work of the Serpent. Within Its Ring of Power the Celestial Couple made love and brought into being all the deities in pairs of two—twins in all things.

On the planet's surface the palm and banana trees swayed in the wind, birds sang, fish swam, and the bush cows roamed in the Garden.

(An original composite)

This is an original rendition of two traditional African myths. This rendition encompasses the creation stories of the Yoruba people of southern Nigeria and the Fon people of Dahomey (Republic of Benin). It attempts to explain in mythological terms the Creation of the Universe, the Birth—all existence as we know it.

In the divining systems of the African diaspora (Ifa and Dilloggun), Wisdom and Guidance are acquired through the deciphering of myths and proverbs. Natural objects such as palm nuts and cowrie shells are cast after the recitation of prayers asking for protection, knowledge, wisdom, and power.

When the natural objects fall on the divining tray, their number and position determine the Odu. An Odu is a sacred letter coded in myths and proverbs. By deciphering the meaning of these, the seeker is instructed in the ways of life (according to an African worldview) and is guided on personal conduct in relation to the issue under consideration.

When one cowrie shell falls on the tray, the Odu is called Okanran (also known as Ocana). Okanran is a fiery letter associated with volcanic eruption and sudden explosions. The accompanying proverb says "The world began with One," and we are told that everything "good" and "bad" was born from this One.

Most modern cosmologists subscribe to a "Big Bang" theory. Suddenly out of the void came a tremendous explosion. It's said that the heat generated in the first fraction of a second was so intense that it cannot be described by any *known* laws of physics.

Physics teaches that the photon, the earliest known manifestation of matter, is both a particle and a wave. This means it has both an expansive (male) and a contractive (female) quality. The theory says that light created by the Big Bang contained all the energy that has ever existed in the universe.

Albert Einstein's famous equation $E = MC^2$ is a quantification (C^2) of matter based on the speed of light. If we reduce the equation to its simplest form (a proverb), it is E = M, Energy = Matter, "from the first burst of Energy all Matter was born."

In Yoruba mythology one of the oldest deities is called *Obatala*. Literally translated the name means "King of the White Cloth," the clouds. King, yes! But Obatala is regarded as having both male and female aspects. And this deity's power is a "Great White Light."

Obatala is credited with creating the World as we know it. And just as all Matter comes from Energy, all forces in Nature (Orisha) evolved from Obatala. The myth tells us that Obatala, in celebrating Creation, rested on a palm tree and became intoxicated from drinking palm wine. The palm tree is the symbol of Iya Mapo (the Goddess of Pottery). She can be understood as the feminine archetype of Form in the Universe. Iya is the cosmic Tree of Life that gives shape to Obatala's creation. She is also symbolized by the snail shell, the expanding spiral, a pattern that occurs in trees, windstorms, galaxies, and the potter's wheel.

The totem for Obatala is the living snail, a symbol of androgynous reproduction. Snails have both male and female reproductive organs, and their mating results in mutual pregnancies. This is symbolic of the dual quality of Light as it gives birth to Matter. Coupled with the geometric proportions of its shell, the snail's androgyny makes it the perfect representation of Primal Procreation.

Those who believe in the notion of "Divine Perfection" may find offensive a myth in which the Creator stops for a drink. But the idea of an unexpected occurrence or mistake is common to African, European, and Native American mythology. Our idea of perfection exists as an archetype in the womb of Potential. When it is transformed into physical reality it is often less than "ideal." Nature is as it is, not as we would like it to be. The very fabric of Creation is the diversity of Nature. No two leaves on any tree are *exactly* the same. Every woman and every man has an ideal (archetype) of a "perfect baby"; when the baby is born, it's often "flawed" in comparison to our ideal.

Obatala, who shapes the child in the womb, is considered to hold in special favor those born with bone malformations and learning disabilities. Worshipers of Obatala are given a taboo against drinking and are advised to be clean and respectful and to practice ethical behavior. Some do. Some don't.

Ibeji

In the African diaspora, polarity in Nature is envisioned as a set of twins called Ibeji; Ibeji can be seen as protons and electrons, man and woman, Earth and Sky. Everything that exists in Nature emerges out of and stands beside its opposite.

In symbolic language, meaning is multilayered. The stars float in the cosmic "Water of Heaven" while the fish swim in the "Water of Earth." In Yoruba myth these are called the domain of Olorun (Owner of the Sky) and the domain of Yemaya-Olokun (Mother of the Deep). Both symbolize the "Waters of the Womb," where the body of the child is formed and the Spirit enters.

So, existence as we know it is male and female, ordered and diverse, spiritual and material—born from the Great One.

The Birth of Gods

In the traditions of the African diaspora the deities represent the Forces of Nature and are personified as male and female.

15

These deities are called *Orisha* by the Yoruba people of south-west Nigeria and *Voudoun* by the Fon people of Dahomey. They are believed to be born from the *Unknowable One*. Their birth and the birth of *Everything Knowable* is the Great Mystery of Manifestation.

Two primal principles generate all that exists. In the Yoruba religion (Ifa/Orisha) these two powers are called *Olodumare* and *Eleda,* born from *Olorun*—the Unknowable One. And in the Dahomean religion (Fa/Voudoun) they are called *Mawu* and *Lisa,* born from *Nana Buluku.*

The Yoruba refer to Olorun as "He"; the Fon refer to Nana as "She." There are subtle differences in the beliefs held about their respective natures.

Olorun is regarded as being beyond comprehension.

The Yoruba . . . believe in the existence of an ALMIGHTY GOD, him they term Olorun, i.e. LORD OF HEAVEN.

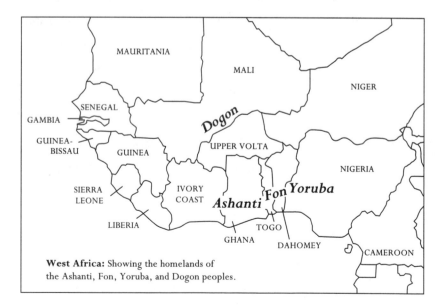

West Africa: Showing the homelands of the Ashanti, Fon, Yoruba, and Dogon peoples.

They acknowledge Him, Maker of heaven and earth, but too exalted to concern Himself directly with men and their affairs, hence they admit the existence of many gods as intermediaries and these they term "Orishas."[1]

Olorun may be addressed in prayer, but no images are made of Him. He has no priests and does not possess human beings.

Nana Buluku, the senior deity of the Dahomean sky pantheon, is regarded as both female and male, and the solitary parent of Mawu and Lisa, the Moon and the Sun.

Little is known of Nana Buluku, who is held to be the parent of Mawu and Lisa. [In] the testimony of natives . . . in the accounts of what ceremonial exists for the worship of Nana Buluku, the name of the Mawu-Lisa group of gods is always coupled with that of the parental deity. Northwest of Abomey lies the village of Dume, where the only shrine to Nana Buluku in all Dahomey is located. Since it was at this place that Nana Buluku resided when on Earth, it was there that this deity had ordered her temple erected, and those who would worship her must go to this place, where alone the proper rites may be carried out. . . . When a priest of Nana Buluku is dispatched from Dume to visit the given temple of Mawu-Lisa he is believed to be guided by the god, so that such a messenger never asks directions, but relies on a "wand of Mawu," which brings him directly to his destination. . . . Yearly, during the dry season, those who have completed their initiation into the cult of the Sky gods make a pilgrimage to Dume to worship at the temple

of Nana Buluku. . . . Into the temple itself only the greatest and most powerful priests of Nana Buluku may enter,
for it is said that one who puts his foot within its confines
"learns how to speak a hundred tongues at once." This god
never departs from Dume, but receives every day from her
children an account of all that has occurred. Mawu comes
to her during the night and Lisa during the day, each bringing full reports of the happenings in the Universe in which
Nana-Buluku, according to the priests of the Sky-cult, is
the senior.[2]

It seems that Nana touched Earth directly in the remote past,
receives a daily report of Her creation's activities, has a temple and
priests, and communicates with them in "a hundred tongues at
once." So, the Celestial Mother of the Voudoun is not as inaccessi-
ble as the Lord of Heaven.

It is common in African belief to regard the "First Cause" of
creation as a remote deity. Such a deity is often depicted in folklore
as being too big or too old to be constantly involved in the concerns of human beings. Most often this Prime Mover brings into
existence many sacred beings who serve as intermediaries between
human beings and the Great One.

In the paragraphs to follow I will use both the Fon and the
Yoruba names of the deities, hyphenated. The Yoruba identify Olodumare and Eleda as male twins,* but their functions in Nature can
be understood as the same polarity expressed in the female-male
twins of the Dahomean pantheon, Mawu-Lisa. It is difficult to speak

* Olodumare is expressed as feminine in some regions of Nigeria.

18

of these Forces in linear terms. In their native cultures, they carried names that were taboo to pronounce. But we must attempt to understand them and to relate to the Wisdom of their symbolism.

Mawu-Olodumare can be seen as the Mother Calabash of Spiritual Essence that sets the pattern for all Creation. Within the Womb of Mawu exist the archetypes that guide and nurture the flow of evolution. Olodumare incubates the Cosmic Egg that gives birth to every newly created level of existence. The Egg is eternal and gestates in a place beyond time and space.

The birth of Matter from Spirit occurs as a function of Time. Matter brings Time into existence by giving it a frame of reference in the cycle of growth and decay. Everything that is, moves out of the Womb of What Could Be into the Present. From the Present it moves back into the Womb of What Was and moves toward the embrace of What Will Be.

The Eternal Present is Lisa-Eleda. He is the Father Seed, the animating principle that sets this flow into motion. He guides Spirit to descend into Matter in the Present. It comes out of the darkness and returns to the darkness. Eleda is constantly supported by the invisible past and the mysterious future.

These twins are the Cosmic Egg and Sperm that give birth to Earth, Air, Fire, and Water, the Voudoun-Orishas. Each represents a particular form of interaction between the Cosmic Egg and Sperm that occurs and recurs at every level of existence.

In the divining system (Ifa-Dilloggun) it is possible to mark the flow of time through the cycle of birth, life, death, and spirit leading to rebirth. There are combinations that include all the symbolic ways in which Egg and Sperm interact. This interaction is called *Du/Odu* and symbolizes the known ways in which Spirit can give birth to the force of nature. The *Odu* occur and recur at every level of existence.

African spirituality represents at least five thousand years of observation, intuitive understanding, and folkloric commentary on the ways in which Spiritual Power manifests in the Material World.

Winter

Mother of the Night

Mother of the Night

I am the Mother of the Night.

The Great Dark Depth, the Bringer of Light.

All that was, that is, that ever shall be,

all that could or should can only come from me.

High above and far below. I am the ebb, I am the flow. The
stars in the sky, the fish in the sea. Every seed, every
stone, every critter is me.

I am the Center, the Beginning, the End. I am without and
I am within. I am the lair, the nest, and the den. I am
the Earth, the Water, and Wind.

The Horned Cow, the many-teated Sow, the Queen bee,
the Mothertree, the Pregnant Womb, the Grain-seed
broom, the candle's wick, the matrix, and woman,
you are my daughter.

Praise and Love to the Mothers of the World.

Praise and Love to the Sisters of the World.

Praise and Love to the Women of the World.

Praise and Love to my daughters.

To the women in the fields, who plow and plant and turn
mill wheels. To those who spin and weave at looms
who make the mats, the cloth and brooms. To those
who sew the royal robes, to those who pierce the
child's earlobes. To those who rub and oil and braid.
To all the Queens and all the Maids.

Praise and Love to my daughters.

To those who nurse babes on their breasts, who carry on
without due rest. Then rise up early as the dawn to
mend the fence and mow the lawn. To those who mix
and stir the pot, to those who bake and clean and
mop, to those who have and who have not.

Praise and Love to my daughters.

Praise and Love to those who seek, to those who know, and
those who speak. To those who smile with tender eyes,
whose wisdom penetrates the lies. To those who sing
and those who cry. For those who fight for right and
die! To those who live to ripe old age, to great-grandma
the family sage. Praise and Love to my daughters.

To those unborn and yet to come, we bid you on with
song and hum. From other worlds and through birth-
water. Come forth child, beloved daughter.

Praise and Love to the Mothers of the World.

Praise and Love to the Sisters of the World.

Praise and Love to the Women of the World.

Praise and Love to my daughters.

L. Teish, original praise-poem for Yemonja, 1992

Blue Mother Moon

Night comes early in Winter. At Moonrise the Earth is quiet and
Nature sleeps beneath Her blanket of Snow. She dreams of the
coming of Spring, the return of the Sun, a time when She will
blush and blossom and birds will sing in Her hair. Tomorrow. Soon.
But tonight She is Blue Mother Moon.

Tonight She embraces the stillness, tonight She exalts the Dark. In the Dreamtime the Moon illuminates the sky. Trees stand shamelessly naked exposing their branches to the wind. The Moon's light casts deep shadows. Humans gaze at Her in wonder and take refuge in their homes.

There before the fireplace we gather. Frosty clouds of breath escape from our mouths. Reverently we lay oak logs and strike a match in honor of the Sun. And comforted we warm our hands as Mother Moon smiles.

We gather our family around us, embrace friends, and make peace with our enemies. We cook life-sustaining porridge and bake breads made of wheat, oats, and rye.

Those who can afford it will flock to warm climates, to Florida or Jamaica, to bask in the Sun.

The unfortunate ones, the homeless people, will wander in the streets. They will freeze, starve, and die, and Blue Mother Moon will cry for Her children.

The truly fortunate, who possess a kind heart, will open their doors and their pockets. Soup kitchens will flourish and the sad eyes of needy children will be brightened by holiday gifts sincerely given. Through mutual help we will survive the Winter.

The Day Her Belly Burst

Night comes early in Winter; the Dark is deep and long. Yet in the stillness of sleep and death, Yemonja gives us Her song. In Her quiet dreaming the hum of the Ocean is heard. In the rushing waters Olokun gives us the Word.

I was there in the beginning
and I'll be there till the end.
In my depths new life is teeming
all that dies will live again.

Yemonja is the Mother of the Deep, the Dream Queen, the
Keeper of Secrets. In the African diaspora She is celebrated in
Winter. Those of us who find ourselves in Brazil, the Caribbean, or
North America are greatly indebted to Her for our protection dur-
ing the Great Darkness, the middle-passage of the slave trade. She
is the Ocean blue.

In Africa, Her place of origin, She is a deity of primal importance. She and Her brother/husband Aganju are the first set of
twins born of Obatala (the White Clouds) and Oduddua (the Black
Goddess of the Earth), the twin sister of Olorun.

Aganju is Lord of the Wilderness and is sometimes associated
with the Volcano. Yemonja is the Mother of the Fish. Together they
are Land and Water.

In the folklore of the Yoruba people Yemonja and Aganju
mated and gave birth to Orungan, the height of the sky.

Orungan, however, had no twin and pursued His mother as a
mate. She was not pleased by His attentions and fled. In the process
She fell backwards and Her belly burst.

> . . . two streams of water gushed from her breasts, and her
> abdomen burst open. The streams from Yemonja's breasts
> joined and formed a lagoon, and from her gaping body
> came the following: Dada (god of vegetables), Shango (god
> of lightning), Ogun (god of iron and war), Olokun (god of
> the sea), Olosa (goddess of the lagoon), Oya (goddess of

the River Niger), Oshun (goddess of the River Oshun), Oba (goddess of the River Oba), Orisha Oko (god of agriculture), Oshosi (god of hunters), Oke (god of the mountains), Aje Shaluga (god of wealth), Shankpana (god of smallpox), Orun (the Sun), and Oshu (the Moon). To commemorate this event, a town was given the name of Ife (distention, enlargement, or swelling up), was built on the spot where Yemonja's body burst open, and became the holy city of the Yoruba-speaking tribes.[3]

Some of these deities will be discussed in greater detail as we progress through the seasons.

We see from this myth that Yemonja is the Mother of the Gods. She is often called the Mother of the Ogun River in Nigeria; and in the Western Hemisphere She is closely associated with another of Her sons—Olokun.

Olokun is the God of the Sea. He is envisioned as a Black man with long flowing hair and mud-fish legs. Legend associates Him with a king who was paralyzed. He dresses royally in coral and lives in a palace at the bottom of the sea.

As the God of Water and Wealth, He is worshiped by fishermen in His holy city, Benin. He is both son and husband to Yemonja but also has other wives: Elusu, the chalk-white mermaid, and Olosa, the Lady of the Lagoon.

Olokun's Challenge

A popular myth of Olokun says that He challenged the Land for its boundaries. Obatala accepted the challenge and sent His mes-

senger Chameleon to summon Olokun. The Lord of the Deep sur-
faced wearing a fine cloth of many colors, but Chameleon was
dressed exactly the same. The God called for His servants to bring
His finest raiment and immediately Chameleon matched Him.
Seven times the Lord of Wealth adorned Himself and seven times
Chameleon became His mirror. Perplexed and humbled by this,
Olokun realized that He could not challenge One whose mere
messenger possessed such power. So the Lord of the Deep receded to
His domain and the land was safe. But, perhaps the whole story
has not been told. Perhaps He absorbed some degree of that power.
For the riches of the Ocean are as wondrous as those of the land,
and the statues of Olokun show Him holding a lizard tightly in
His hands.

(A returned tale, L. Teish, 1993)

Yemonja and Olokun may be mother and son, husband and wife, or one gynandrous deity.

They are the salt waters of the Earth. They are the weight of the planet, the substance from which the clouds are made. In Their depth the power of the Earth resides quietly in Winter.

Their domain is rich and wondrous, populated by mystical beings who work with Them to maintain the world of the deep.

Yemonja-Olokun, the beauty of dreams, comes to us shimmering like moonlight on the waves. She comes whispering secrets, sweet and sinister: today is forgotten, ancient memory returns.

Back in the "before time," in the darkness, Intelligence mated with Power. And in Her pregnant belly the single cell evolved, creating seaweed, hydra, and fish. All the power that was, that is, that ever shall be, is there waiting for you to dream it, to bring it forth from the potentiality of Winter to the blossoming reality of Spring.

Sleep, and in that sleeping, wake. Go into the darkness and once there, see the light. It is the shining eye of the serpent Damballah Hwedo. He knows the secrets, all that has been thought and felt. All that has been lost is found in the glimmer of His eyes.

Olokun, the keeper of dreams, sends our genes to face the light of day. And walking carefully in the path of the Moon, we humans may find our way.

⌣·

The waters of the Ocean touch the shores of every continent and surround the Islands of the World. The Divine Daughter Oshupa, the Moon, also affects the tides of the Ocean and gives beauty to the night sky. Together the Moon and the Ocean keep the liquid dance of the planet going; roots and bulbs keep growing, and women's monthly Moonblood keeps flowing. The Spring of Life, the possibility of Birth, begins with Woman's Moonblood and the end of it is signaled by Menopause and the Winter of Her life.

Oriki Yemonja

Iba Yemonja Awoyo
Iba Yemonja Okudte
Iba Yemonja K'onla
Iba Yalode
Yemonja a'tara magwa
onoboye ba me.
Ma ja kiki won aje
Yemonja fun mi omo.
Adupe. Ase.

Praise to the crown of the rainbow.

Praise to the coral reef.

Praise to the foam on the wave.

Praise to the Mother.

The beauty of the Ocean is my salvation.

Respect to the power of the Mothers.

I thank the Mother of the fishes for giving me children.

So be it.

Yemonja-Olokun is the Great Progenitor of human life. Olokun is the Evolutionary Father, the keeper of genes who directs the development of the species. He gives us our ancestral heritage, our characteristics, our predispositions, and our limitations.

Yemonja is the Great Mother. She is the Principle of Existence. She is the pregnant belly, the nurturer, the developer. She brings us into the world, bathes and feeds us, and helps us discover who we are and what we are to become.

Nobody Knows What's at the Bottom of the Ocean

In 1981 I received an Ikoko Olokun (a sacred vessel) in a ceremony in Oakland, California. The rite was performed according to the standard guidelines used in North America. It was explained to me that there were "greater secrets" to Olokun, but that those had been lost during the slave period. I was then told that some Caribbean Island priests (those of Cuba and Puerto Rico, but not Haiti) regarded the force of Olokun as being "too powerful" to be fully ritualized. Years later I witnessed greater secrets and experienced great power at a full initiation for Olokun in West Africa. Since then I have enjoyed a deeper intimacy and greater manifestation in my work with that Orisha.

My American ceremony was good, and divination revealed that the deity was pleased to be entering my home. I was also told that I could serve others by involving myself with issues of health and poverty. I was not yet a priest, but Olokun had agreed to be my power source in these matters.

I took my Ikoko home and meditated before the altar for many nights, asking for guidance on how I was to serve others in this way. I was told to celebrate the anniversary of my ceremony (December 30) every year in a public ritual where invited guests could wash their troubles away. This I did for several years.

Having Olokun gave more meaning to Winter, a season that I am not particularly fond of. Christmas had lost its meaning for me long ago. Kwanzaa, a uniquely African American holiday, had provided me with an expression of culture but did not contain enough of the "spiritual" for my needs. The presence of Olokun brought in the spirit and expanded the parameters of kinship to include Haiti and Brazil.

When my Brazilian sisters performed their ritual at midnight on New Year's Eve on the beaches of Rio, I danced with them before my altar in Oakland.

One year the theme of my ritual was a popular proverb, "Nobody knows what's at the bottom of the ocean." The Full Moon in Cancer of that year was a total eclipse.

At the time I was cofacilitating a women's spirituality group—the Daughters of the Gelefun. The group was composed of twenty-one women of different races, ages, and lifestyles. The women

gathered at my home and began building a shrine. We started at
9:00 P.M. and ended at sunrise. The shrine was built under the influence of that Blue Moon.

After clearing the dining room of all furniture, we covered the
floor with palm mats and canopied the ceiling with thirty yards of
sand-colored fabric embossed with large blue scallop shells. We
brought in fresh seaweed from the Pacific and draped it on the
walls (it was later returned to the Ocean). Next we placed a bowl
of blue water and a white candle in the center of the room and
called the Ocean Goddess by Her many names—Mami-Wata, Ku-
napipi, Beautiful Shell, Tiamat. And then the magic happened.

We created from shells and sand, from paper and cloth, from
wax and bread dough, in neutral tones and in blazing color. In the
shrine we created an underwater world: a mountain range, an
erupting volcano, a forest and a sea-fruit garden, a zoo, a city and a
solar system. There were images of goddesses from everywhere
and a banquet of seafood fit for a queen.

Exhausted, the women went home to rest. Everyone would return elegantly dressed to start the ritual at 7:00 P.M. I slept, satisfied and proud of our work.

At five o'clock I walked into my kitchen and saw the mess we
had made from cooking all night. I rattled a few dishes, reached for
the soap, and turned on the hot water. The faucet crumbled in my
hands! Hot water shot straight up to the ceiling and rained down
on me as a full cloud of steam rolled through the room. I ran out
the back door screaming and pulling my clothes away from my
skin. The boy next door turned something outside and shut off all
the water. When we went in the house the kitchen floor was
flooded. While I mopped up the water, he fixed the sink. After I

31

washed the dishes I changed clothes and prepared to meet my
guests.

When the first daughter arrived she noted that the dining room
floor was dry but the walls were dripping from the steam. We both
laughed as we accepted the answer to our riddle. "What's on the
bottom of the ocean?" Water, and that's for sure.

Power Is Her Name

Whenever I speak of Yemonja, meaning is layered. Yemonja is the
Ocean Herself, the Primal Intelligence that existed on the planet
in its Winter, before Life developed in the Garden. Yemonja is the
quality of nurturance found in plants, animals, and human beings.
She is the call to care, the urge to provide. She is milk-filled
breasts and loving hands. These qualities are personified in folklore. She is envisioned as a Black-skinned mermaid with long seaweed hair, paisley eyes, and voluptuous angular breasts. She has
many names.

As *A'taramagwa* She is the beautiful Queen of the Deep Waters.
As *Awoyo* She resides in the middle of the Ocean, where She protects sailors and fishermen. *Yemonja Asesu* is a whirlpool in the waters. She's the One who swallowed the *Titanic* for lunch. *Ayaba* is
the anchor, the stabilizing force that allows us to float on the waves.
Ogunte violently slams Her waves against the mountains. This warrior woman has a machete in Her pocket, and Ogun the Warlord is
Her consort. *Mayelewo* sits at the water's edge, eats black-eyed peas
and cornbread, and combs Her hair with the trees in the woods.
Ololodi walks so closely with Her daughter-sister Oshun that they
are regarded as One. Here the Ocean and the River meet. These

are the waters of Temperance used to balance the bitter and the sweet. And *Yemonja-Olokun,* the dream team, wraps us in the light of Blue Mother Moon and takes us safely through the Winter.

Power is the name of Yemonja.

The Winter Solstice

Winter officially begins with the Solstice on December 21. It is the *longest night* of the year. Thereafter night will diminish and day will increase until they are equally balanced at the Spring Equinox. On March 21, day begins to increase and continues its ascendancy until June 21, the Summer Solstice, the *longest day* of the year. Day will then yield its power until these twins are equals again at the Autumn Equinox on September 21. This is the Great Dance: Birth, Life, and Death leading to Rebirth. This is the Natural Cycle: Gestation, Growth, Fullness, and Harvest.

Much of the ancient symbolism of the Winter Solstice has been absorbed into the rituals of Christmas. In that tradition the Sun is symbolized as the Son of God, Jesus, the Christ. In other cultures the reigning King holds that position. We also find a Goddess figure who brings us out of the Darkness into the Light. Usually She is the Mother-Lover of the Sun-King, but sometimes She is the Sun itself. We will take a closer look at the Feminine Sun in the chapter on Summer.

Some of these Light Celebrations begin before the official Solstice and continue throughout the Winter. They are numerous and varied, serious and colorful, simple and complex. Although sometimes found in warm climates, they are most important in cold countries that rely heavily on the Sun for their survival.

A Litany of Light

December 13: In Sweden there is a celebration called the Luciada-gen. The eldest daughter in the family adorns herself in a white robe with a red sash. She wears a crown of lighted candles on her head and serves her elders breakfast in bed. During this time there is a procession for St. Lucy.

December 16: For eight nights Mexican villagers hold *posadas.* They visit each other's homes, singing and asking for entry. This is a reenactment of Joseph and Mary's search for shelter on the night her child was born.

December 17–24: These days marked the Roman Saturnalia, when the social order was reversed. Masters and slaves traded places in honor of Saturn the taskmaster and ruler of the astrological sign Capricorn. The Goddess of Opulence also received a banquet in Her honor at this time. In Europe Christmas Eve was the "Night of the Mothers" and Christmas was "Child's Day."

Inscriptions are known from Roman times in Germany, Holland, and Britain in honor of a group of female beings called "the Mothers. [They were] evidently associated with fertility and with the protection of health and home."[4]

December 21: The official beginning of Winter is celebrated by many pagan practices, which include lighting bonfires or Yule logs to entice the return of the Sun. Evergreens, plants whose vitality survives the withdrawal of Earth's energy in Winter, are decorated in honor of the Tree of Life. Kissing under the mistletoe, singing, and food sharing are all Solstice practices.

The native people of Guatemala also have an interesting tradition.

On this day the Mayan Indians . . . honor the sun god they worshipped long before they became Christians. Every year, for the dangerous palo voladare, or flying pole dance, three men climb to a platform at the top of a 50 foot pole. There, two of the men wind one of the long ropes attached to the pole around one foot. As the third man beats a drum and plays a flute, both jump off the platform. Slowly the ropes unwind, and the two dancers descend. If they land on their feet, the sun god will be so pleased that he'll start shining a bit longer every day.[5]

December 22: In South Africa the King of Swaziland was regarded as the Sun personified. On this day his warriors danced and chanted around his compound, enticing him to come forth from a long seclusion.

December 24–25: Celebrations on Christmas Eve and Christmas Day vary according to the sect of Christianity to which the celebrants belong. Usually they include all the Solstice practices named above with the addition of Nativity scenes, caroling, and midnight mass or other church services.

December 26–January 1: Kwanzaa is an African American holiday first observed in the United States in 1966. It is based on the East African celebration of "first fruit." During this time a candle is lit each night in honor of the Seven African Principles. They are: Umoja (Unity), Kujichagulia (self-determination), Ujima (collective work), Ujamaa (shared economics), Nia (life purpose), Kuumba (creativity), and Imani (faith). At this time many celebrants give up their slave names and adopt meaningful African names.

New Year's Eve: On New Year's Eve people use various means to dispel the influence of the old year. These include blowing horns, which cleans away the ghosts, and smashing crockery that held grain (symbolizing the spirit of Winter).

Many people step outside and fire their handguns at midnight. Whatever the symbolism, it certainly serves to let you know how many guns there are on your block. So pay attention! Usually all this noise is followed by some form of divination or luck-casting on New Year's Day. The passage of Time is symbolized by a bearded old man with a sickle who gives way to a newborn baby.

A European Holiday

November 1992 found me romping joyfully through the city of Amsterdam. I'd been in Holland a few weeks and needed another travel bag to accommodate the books and clothes I'd bought and the gifts I'd been given. When traveling I always buy a piece of cloth indigenous to the area and a book of regional folklore. That way I take a piece of the "real people" home with me.

Until this particular day I'd spent most of my time in the countryside. I still wasn't accustomed to the flatlands, but I'd found the sugar beets, windmills, and old castles intriguing. In Amsterdam, I was enchanted by the statues of Hermes and Poseidon overlooking the canals, seduced by vendors selling cheese and Belgian lace, and flattered by an occasional flirtatious smile.

One of my companions surmised that the bag I wanted could be found only in one of the major department stores. So we turned a corner and suddenly I was confronted by Dutch Christmas decorations.

Christmas decorations in November have always irritated me. The tendency to project a Winter holiday into the Fall season seems to me unnatural. In the United States stores begin their Christmas advertising as early as the day after Halloween. Only crass commercialism rushes us to the next buying frenzy.

As I walked with my friends from one store to the next, I became aware of the presence of a Black figure in their holiday decorations. I'd met many Black people from Suriname living in Holland, but this figure did not reflect any of that culture.

Some displays depicted a stylish Black high-fashion mannequin while others used the image of a pollywog—a bug-eyed black doll with big white or red lips. These made me think of blackfaced minstrels. In the minstrel shows white men put burnt cork on their faces and acted out outrageous stereotypes of Black people. In these shows we were always depicted as lazy, fearful, and ignorant. When Black performers sought the American stage they were forced to blacken their natural faces and perform an imitation of an imitation of themselves.

Curious and a bit insulted, I began taking pictures of the Black figure. Eventually my companions noticed my interest and introduced me to this character. His name is Black Peter and he's Santa Claus's hit man.

At first I thought they were pulling my leg, but a little research affirmed this piece of information.

In much of Europe, and particularly in Holland, the main fun takes place on St. Nicholas Eve, 5 December. According to the story, St. Nicholas, who was a Bishop, comes each year in a ship from Spain, riding a white horse, to visit every child. To those who are good he will give a gift of sweets or biscuits, and those who have been bad get a light smack with a bunch of birch twigs. Children set out a clog or shoe beside the fireplace containing some hay, bread and a carrot to reward the saint's horse, in the hope that his assistant, Black Pete, will leave a present, rather than delivering a smack, or worse still, wrapping the really bad children up in the empty sack he carries and transporting them away to Spain as captives.[6]

Christmas is a time of drama, music, and pageantry. "Scrooge," the *Nutcracker* ballet, and Dr. Seuss's *How the Grinch Stole Christmas* are seasonal standards.

In Europe and the United States the mummers' plays are also staged at this time. Traditionally, the mummers' theme is a battle between a White Knight and a Black Villain usually depicted as being of Turkish (Moslem) or Moorish descent. Of course the White Knight (the Christian) always wins. I ponder whether this is a reenactment of the battle between Day and Night or dramatized emotional resentment over the Moorish conquest.

In any event, I am *not* enamored with this holiday as it is celebrated in the popular culture. I am, however, very fortunate to be able to create meaningful rituals for the season.

Those of us who are disenchanted with the racism, gender-biased symbolism (a baby boy and three wise men), and crass commercialism of the season can take hope in the celebration of Yemonja-Olokun and the other Water Spirits at this time of year.

The waters of the Ocean touch the shores of every continent; we are all born in the salty waters of Woman's womb, and we all dream.

Celebrating the Deep

The Great Waters are celebrated in many ways. In the African diaspora, the Owners of the Waters are honored between December 21 and January 1. The ceremony for *Imanje*—which takes place on the beach of Rio de Janiero—is probably the best known of these celebrations. In Cuba She is called *Yemaya,* and in Haiti *Agwe Taroyo* is the Ocean deity. They carry different names but all have their roots in the ceremonies for the Water Spirits *Olokun* and *Mami-Wata* that originate in West Africa, in Dahomey, Togo, and Nigeria.

Mami-Wata

In Togo and Ghana the Woman of the Waters is Mami-Wata. She is envisioned as a mermaid. Often She is pictured as chalk white.

Some historians claim that the mermaid image came to Africa on the bow of European ships. But others believe that this is simply a Europocentric racist interpretation. "The figures made to represent Mami are doll-like, pale beautiful and transfigured; white—not to depict Europeans, but to stress the state of pale enrapture of her divine-spiritlike existence."[7] She carries a trident and a golden dagger, and Her husband Papa Densu is believed to have come from India.

African spirituality is all-encompassing; it tends to accept that which works, to identify similarities, and to integrate seemingly disparate elements. So many of the spiritual traditions of the diaspora reflect complex mixtures: the original culture, the colonizers' culture, and that of other people imported to the area—African, European, and East Indian. But let it be clear that any people who live near the ocean are likely to perceive it as peopled by creatures who express the marine origin of human existence.

Mamissi

The cult of *Mami-Wata* is a female affair, predominantly, though there are men who participate in Her worship. Female worshipers called *Mamissis* tend to be childless and find prestige in the culture through devotion to the Mermaid. She brings Her devotees power and wealth.

One is called to the service of Mami through dreams. The Mermaid appears in the dream with Her snakes and calls the person to initiation. Her feast, celebrated on December 21, marks the anticipation of the new season. This ceremony celebrates the end of the year. Now the old fetishes are stored away and the new ones are introduced.

In *Voodoo: Africa's Secret Power* Gert Chessi describes a feast he attended in Anecho, Togo.

> White-painted women, heavily hung with chains, parade in long lines. They embody the gods, they *are* the gods to whom the feast is dedicated. At first there are thirty, then a hundred, then hundreds. . . . Among them the chiefs, dignified with white caps, cut and sewn like fish-scales. Unbelievably fat women push in. Their huge breasts hang far down over their wraparound skirts, their necks are heavy with chains, heavy glass, and stone chains, but also silver and gold jewelry. . . .

Chessi describes the transvestite devotees:

> Two transvestites are also here, now hung around with silver. They wear short brocade skirts, and white spectacles are painted around their eyes. Their naked upper bodies

and legs are painted with kaolin in a longitudinal pattern of stripes like those of the women. . . .

The master of ceremonies enters the dancing floor. He welcomes the guests, urges them to sing, and announces the rules. Then the drummer begins to beat their rhythms, the crowd starts with ecstatic incantation, the women beat their upper bodies with their palms. You can feel the vibration in the air. . . . After a few minutes the first trances begin.[8]

From here the ceremony progresses to the beach. Like the worshipers of Imanje in Brazil, Mami-Wata's women carry offerings down to the sea. There they stand in the surf and meditate, sing, and dance. There they await the call of the Mermaid. Perhaps it is the curve of a wave or a figure seen in the mist. Perhaps it is a reflection of light on the water or the whisper of shifting sand. But something is perceived and the mystery unfolds. The women hear the call of the Mermaid and are pulled by the tide of the Ocean. They throw themselves into the Ocean; by the hundreds they plunge into the salty waters of the Great Womb. They pray for Power, for Vision; they lose themselves in the vastness of the Sea. Many of the women cannot swim and are caught in the rhythm of the water. Fully dressed young men dive in to save them from the call of the dangerous Goddess.

Many of the aspects of Mami-Wata and Her service have been maintained with a twist in the Western Hemisphere. For example, Brazilian paintings of Imanje often depict Her as white-skinned and slender instead of full-bodied. African sculptors often present Her as large with paisley eyes and long angular breasts. In Cuba Yemaya

41

is rumored to be the "Mother of Gay Men." I say "rumored" because no one has ever cited the Odu (the sacred letter) to substantiate this office. And in Her priesthood one can find men and women of both sexual persuasions. One can speculate that She has been so called because of the unusual reproductive possibilities found in the Ocean. In the deep we find both asexual (simple cell division) and cross-sexual (the pregnancy of the *male* seahorse) reproduction.

It is the practice in several African rituals to wear clothing sacred to the deity being worshiped. Thus a male devotee in service to a female deity would dress like the Goddess and a female in service to a male deity would dress like the God. Interrelationship including androgyny is recognized and celebrated and ritual cross-dressing may be done even as animals and plants.[9]

In the divining system of Dilloggun, the sacred letter in which the Ocean Goddess speaks always directs the seeker to examine the content of her dreams for spiritual messages. I have encountered many people whose dreams have led them to the door of initiation, and I myself have had encounters with the Mermaid. Contrary to Walt Disney's innocent depiction of Her, I know the Mermaid as a powerful, alluring, and sometimes dangerous Goddess who both nourishes and consumes Her children.

Agwe Taroyo

In Haiti the ceremony for *Agwe Taroyo* reflects the worship of Olokun of Benin. As with Mami, a strong attraction to water or dreams of swimming in the Ocean are signs that initiation to Olokun is forthcoming. Devotees of Olokun are given to prophetic dreaming, deep reflection, and in some cases seizures similar to epilepsy. The devotees of Agwe, like those of Olokun, perform elaborate water ceremonies.

> Services for Agwe take place beside the sea (sometimes on the edge of a lake or river) and his effigy—a miniature boat—is then carried in procession. His favorite food and drink are put on a float, a blue and white boat. The boat is decorated with streamers. Drum rhythms are played and devotees dance. Offerings are made in the Ocean and devotees leave without looking back. This is followed by a possession in which people are overcome with memory of their marine nature and want to jump into the sea.[10]

Benin Dream

Ironically, one of my most profound experiences with Olokun involved not the water, but the Moon.

In 1989 while I was in Benin City, Nigeria, I attended the drumming session for an Olokun initiation.

At the initiate's request, I'd been allowed to visit him in his solitude. The officiating priestesses lived in a cave of sorts, but the area housing the initiate was immaculate; the earth floor was covered with palm mats, and the mats were covered with white cloth. During my visit the initiate was covered in *efun* (white chalk) from head to toe, including his eyeballs! He was unfocused, spoke slowly, and said he had been dreaming nonstop for an eternity (actually it was seven days).

After I had been there awhile, I sneezed. The officiating priestess entered the room carrying an herb broom. She promptly cleaned the initiate, then swept the atmosphere and threw the broom out. My visit was over, but she invited me to attend the drumming ceremony that was to take place outside her cave the next night.

I arrived late in the evening, my head covered in a white eyelet *gele*. I wore white shoes and carried a small white clutch purse. This I knew was proper attire for such a ceremony.

My driver proudly led me to the seat of honor, which had been reserved for me. I sat quietly, determined to observe every aspect of the ceremony.

The participants began to gather. As I recall, four drummers came carrying small tublike drums that looked like the East Indian tabla but produced a distinctly different sound. They were followed by at least thirty *shekere* players, all women, who began immediately to make rushing sounds with their instruments. The congregation, a cast of hundreds, made a circle around the swept-dirt center. Everyone's body was painted with white chalk. After about half an hour, a priestess entered and blew white powder around the circle. She raised her arms as if lifting weights, and leaned left and right as part of the invocation to the four directions. Once sacred space was established, she let out a call and a procession began. In the procession were the priestesses who had officiated over the initiation. They were dressed in costumes made of red and white cloth in various proportions and sprinkled with cowrie shells. The initiate was in the middle of the procession. Now the drums started and the women began to display the initiate and to teach him to dance. I tried to watch the steps.

Eventually the first priestess walked over to me and blew a handful of white powder directly into my face. Unwillingly I began to tremble from the inside and tears rolled down my cheeks. I became aware of my driver tugging at my purse and shoes. "You must go and dance," he said. I shook my head no in an attempt to clear my blurring vision. "Yes," my driver said, "this thing is happening to you . . . you must go and dance now. . . ." I wanted to sit and observe, but the priestess returned and blew another handful of powder into my face.

I remember a resounding cry and a bolt of energy as if lightning had struck me in my spine. I have no memory of moving from point A to point B, only of being there in the center of the circle, feeling my legs moving beneath me and my chest and hips gyrating.

I heard a voice above my head ask, "Who is that dancing?" I lifted my eyes to the night sky, then saw and felt the Full Moon descending into my mouth, squeezing itself down my throat and into my belly.

I became aware that I had been moved to an inner chamber, a place where life-sized figures made of chalk were somehow painted or inlaid with gold. I looked around, trying to identify the sculptures. I recognized Shango, the God of Thunder in male and female form, erect and pregnant. Before I could see much more the priestess grabbed my jaws and pushed my lips forward into a fish mouth. I knew what this meant. This is the way I'd been taught to give medicine to babies. With the lips pursed in this manner it was *almost impossible* to reject the substance now being poured down my throat. Oh but I tried. Water and leaves and grit found their way into my belly.

Then they removed my gele and again there was a great cry. They called the name of the Thunder deity because a few days before, the women of a distant village had braided my hair in the style worn by devotees of Shango (He is my Father, by the way). I was washed from head to toe; then they smeared me with chalk and drew lines on my face and body. My crisp white eyelet clothing was now streaked with chalk and bits of green leaves.

As I looked around me, people moved in the dark, their Black faces covered in white chalk, their eyes fully opened, staring at me. I thought I was in a Fellini movie or a painted mime drama. I felt as if these people and I were hovering somewhere between the worlds.

Then the priestesses began making predictions for me. Some of them were worrisome, some of them wonderful. All have proved to be true.

As a result of all these rituals I feel that the natural confluence between the River (my Goddess, Oshun) and the Ocean (Yemonja-Olokun) has been enhanced in my consciousness. My dreams are often prefaced with an image of me running through a house, chased by a great ocean wave. At a point I allow the wave to wash over me and then my dreams for the night begin. I have found these dreams to be prophetic, symbolic, and instructive.

A full discussion of the mystery of Dreams goes beyond the scope of this book, but at this chapter's end you will find a tidbit to enhance your dreaming. Every year when I perform my ritual for Olokun, I remember my Benin dream.

In Winter when the night is long, the Earth consolidates Her power. At this time we can look within, explore the depths of our psyches, receive the prophecy, and prepare ourselves for the Promise of Spring.

Happy New Year?

New Year's Day occurs in the dead of Winter. So why is it *new*? The ecological season does not truly change until the Spring Equinox on March 21; then the world is new. Similarly, one minute after *midnight* is called morning. Why? For me morning occurs when the Sun rises at dawn.

For many years these time designations escaped my comprehension and actually aggravated me. They seem to be great examples of the human tendency (especially in Western culture) to mechanize Time, to try to force Nature into our own limited existence. Why are we in such a hurry? And just where does it all lead?

On New Year's Day some people drink and drive. They cut and shoot each other, or waste the day and their resources in a show of conspicuous consumption. Often the day after New Year's, people are severely depressed and suicidal.

On January 2, 1990, a friend and I were driving to a nearby shopping center to pick up a few items. We came to a four-way intersection, a crossroads regulated only by a flashing yellow light. The cars coming from the north, east, and south were stopped, and I stopped in the west. Being the last to arrive, I waited for the other cars to move first. But each of them started to move, rolled less than a foot, and stopped. This was done several times in an irregular pattern. I realized that we each thought the others were high or drunk and we were afraid to move. A man in a black car pulled up behind me and honked his horn angrily. Then I broke out of the energy pattern. As I was crossing the bridge the black car pulled alongside me. I smiled and asked the brother how he was doing. His answer startled me. With a disgusted look on his face he shook his head, nodded to the sky, and said, "The mean motherf—ker let me live another day." Then he took off at breakneck speed. I realized that this man was talking about God and I feared that his death invocation might manifest in the next crossroad.

In the years that I have lived in the San Francisco Bay Area I've witnessed an increased consciousness about alternative New Year's activities. There have been lakeside vigils for the homeless, driver assistance programs for the bar-hoppers, and all-night sing-alongs for the churchgoers. More and more, people have decided to focus on safety and a worthy cause. Perhaps there is hope.

On New Year's Day many people make resolutions. In order to make resolutions we examine the mistakes and disappointments of the old year. We delve into the dreams that we have for the future. Then we clarify our priorities, declare our intentions, and affirm a positive outcome through a commitment to action. Resolutions are an attempt to prophesy the coming year. They are *will-directed* prophecy.

In the African diaspora there is a tradition of divining for the coming year. Divination may be done for individuals, groups, or the world. In addition to our own divination, my extended family receives predictions for the world from Oyotunji village in South Carolina and from Ile Ife, Nigeria.

African divination is both *will-directed* and *destiny-directed* prophecy. Palm nuts, kola nuts, or cowrie shells are cast to determine what natural occurrences (earthquakes, heat waves) and what human tendencies (fear, communion) are most likely to manifest in the coming year. We ask, What do the deities have in store for us and how are we to conduct ourselves?

The predictions are made and the diviner prescribes various rituals to be performed throughout the year in order to receive blessings and avert danger. In this way the yearly calendar may be set during the first week of the New Year.

To understand and use the guidelines given in divination it is essential to examine the nature of Elegba the Divine Messenger. In the folktale recorded earlier, the Son chased His Mother, Yemonja. She fell and Her body burst. A number of deities are said to have come from Her issue. In this version of the story, however, Elegba is not named.

Another story features an unnamed Goddess who roamed the infinite darkness of space in the beginning of time. It's said (I have not seen the story written anywhere) that She became so lonely that Her belly began to rumble; then it exploded and out came a spark of light, Elegba.

Among Yoruba practitioners the identity of the Mother of Elegba is debated. Some insist that She is Oya, the Queen of the Winds of Change and Lightning; others say that Yemonja is Mother of All the Gods. Naturally I would credit Oshun with birthing the trickster. Others simply say that this Goddess is so old and remote that Her name need not be called. The debate is moot. It is sufficient to say that Elegba is the spark of light (born in Okanran) that comes from the Great Dark Mother.

Elegba's energy functions in Nature and in human nature in three important ways: as Trickster-Magician, as Linguist, and as Enforcer.

The Trickster-Magician: Elegba has often been referred to as the trickster. This designation tends to invoke the image of a clown or joker. While this deity is associated with humor and the unexpected, His function is far greater.

Elegba is the Master of the Crossroads, the Gatekeeper who stands between the Material and the Spiritual, the Visible and the Invisible, between Existence and Oblivion.

The Great Womb contains pure potential. Out of Her darkness the elements of Creation (Earth, Water, Fire, and Air) must come together in various combinations to create reality as we know it.

Elegba, who is associated with the penis, is the spark of light in the Big Bang, the principle of Okanran that activates the Cosmic Egg and through the *trick of perception* causes these elements to come together in a particular fashion. Any incident may be perceived by one person as a challenge, opportunity, or valuable insight, whereas another person will see a problem, an accident, or a mistake. Each will then create, maintain, or destroy according to his or her perception. Elegba is the Messenger of Destiny and of Chance—of that which is predetermined (Natural Law) and that which is to be determined (Volition).

The Linguist: Elegba is the Linguist of the Gods. He stands in the Crossroads between the right and left brain, allowing intellect and intuition to interact and to communicate that interaction. For example, because He is the Linguist Elegba is always addressed first in ritual. If I wish to speak to Yemonja, Elegba translates my human language into "water-talk" and then interprets Yemonja's water-talk into human language. She and I then understand each other, agree, and take mutually beneficial action. The ritual is born. In this way Elegba facilitates between Will and Destiny.

The Enforcer: The true laws of Nature will and must manifest. The Sun will not stop shining nor will the Ocean dry up because you will it so. On the other hand, you have a choice to sunbathe or not, to swim or not. Choice requires decision, and decision requires that we take responsibility for the consequences of our choice. Sometimes we are faced with difficult decisions that defy logic. At these times the wise choice is to ask for guidance. Sometimes something illogical or seemingly irrelevant to the question happens and we decide. At these times we say that Elegba the Enforcer has kicked us out of the Crossroads of Indecision.

On New Year's Day we stand in the Crossroads between the Past and the Future. We ponder where we've been, where we are, and where we hope to go. We invoke Elegba, consult our oracles, receive guidance and direction, set the calendar, and celebrate. In many communities a drum ceremony is held in celebration of Elegba on New Year's Day.

In anticipation of performing rituals throughout the year, we will begin with the creation of a ritual space in your home.

⌣· *The Winter Rituals* ·⌣

Creating Sacred Space

You can begin the important work of creating a sacred space by building altars for the four directions in a chosen room of the house. This should be the room in which the other rituals for the year will take place. By designating a ritual room you can have privacy from the eyes and comments of disapproving relatives whose visits may be obligatory during the holidays. If you are fortunate enough to belong to an Earth-centered community and free of such imposition, by all means use the entire house as your ritual space. Begin by cleaning the space.*

Cleaning the Ritual Room

Look around your environment. What plant is blooming abundantly? In many places the trees will be bare and not many flowers will be in bloom. Whatever is still growing contains the strongest Earth energy available at this, Her time of withdrawal and rest.

* For a thorough housecleaning, see *Jambalaya*.

Go to the place where plants still live. Take an offering of whole fruit or a compost mixture such as eggshells and coffee grounds.

Choose the tree, shrub, or flower bush and announce your name and your intention. Your intention is to give nourishment so that you may receive cleanliness. Place your offering at the base of the plant, then pull up or cut off enough plant material to make a broom. Use your judgment. If the plant removal creates a hole in the Earth, put your offering in the hole and cover it with soil. If you are taking branches from a tree, place your offering at the base of the tree or inside openings in the tree bark, if there are any.

Sweeping the Walls: Take the plant material home. Before making your broom, please pinch off a piece of the plant material and store it in a cool dry place. You will need this later.

Now tie the rest of the plant material into a bundle with a strip of white cloth. Begin at the door of your ritual room (the inside) and sweep the walls at the corners from the ceiling to the floor.

It is best to start at the top of the corner, where the wall meets the ceiling, and make one brisk stroke down the corner's crease. Do this in every corner of the ritual room. If Earth has been generous enough to give you a large bundle, feel free to sweep all the rooms of your house. If greenery is sparse in your area, be grateful for the opportunity to clean your ritual room. Put the used plant broom in the garbage can or in your compost box.

Sweeping the Floor: With your regular straw broom you will sweep the floor of your ritual room. *Do not use a vacuum cleaner.* If you have a carpet, dip the tip of your broom in lightly salted water and sweep the carpet vigorously. Begin in the corners of your ritual room. Sweep the dirt from the corners in every direction to the center of the floor. Pick up this debris and put it in a brown paper bag. Store it. It will be used later for a very important ritual. Rinse your broom, beat the water out of it, and stand it in a corner, *brush end up* in its storage place. Later, when the broom is completely dry, spray it with a nice perfume.

Smudging: Prepare a mixture for smudge. I recommend a combination of cedar, sage, tobacco, and lavender flowers. Sprinkle a little bay rum, Florida water, or crisp-scented cologne on the mixture and set the mixture aflame in a cast-iron pot. It will flare up, so have the pot cover ready. Smother the flame with the pot cover, then walk to each corner of your ritual room. Run a stream of smoke up the corner crease while raising the pot. When this is done, let the burning contents cool. Be sure to stir the ashes and let them cool completely. Place the smudge ashes in the same bag with the dirt from the floor. Store the bag in a safe place.

Cleaning with Water: Take the piece of greenery pinched from your cleansing broom earlier. Put about a gallon of water in a pot on the stove. When the water reaches the boiling point, cut the fire off and throw the greenery into the pot. Now place four *stones,* four *coins,* and four *seashells* in the pot. Quickly pass four *feathers* through the steam rising from the pot. Lay them aside. Now cover the pot and let it stand. When it's cool, remove the greenery and place it in the bag with the dirt and ashes. Take the other objects out of the pot and put them aside to dry.

Put the cleansing tea in your plant sprayer. Then spray the corners of your ritual room. Begin in the center of the corner's crease. Spray from the center up, then from the center down. Be sure the spout is adjusted to a fine mist. Then walk to the center of the room and spray a fine mist toward each direction.

Building the Altars

You will need four small tables to build the altars on. If your space is limited, use one large table. You may use crates, boxes, or other hard flat surfaces (such as a desk or a piano top).

Cleaning and Preparing the Altar Tables: Take the remaining tea (made above) and sponge the surfaces clean of any dust. You will need a piece of cloth for each altar table or section. One yard of cotton should do nicely for each altar. I recommend the following colors: yellow for the East, red for the South, blue for the West, and white for the North.

Blessing the Cloth: Hold each piece of cloth in your hands, securing the four corners. Kiss each corner of the cloth and expel breath so that you make the sound *HA!* coming from the depths of your root in the creative center of your body (uterus, pubis). Then wave the cloth vigorously over the altar table and surrounding area so that it makes a popping sound. Be sure to turn in each of the four directions above each of the four tables. This means you will pop the four cloths four times each for a total of sixteen times. After clearing the air around each table (by popping the cloth), lay the cloth on the appropriate table.

Placing the Candles: You will need four candles and four oils in the following combinations: yellow candle and Attraction oil; red candle and Fire of Passion; blue candle and Meditation or Prophetic Dream oil; white candle and Success oil.*

Place a candle holder in the center of each altar table. Moisten the palms of your hands with the appropriate oil for the candle you

---

* These can be purchased at a local Botanica or made at home. For recipes see *Jambalaya*.

are charging. Begin with the North candle, then go on to the East, South, and West candles. Take the North candle in hand, holding it in the center. Oil the candle from the center down and the center up, asking on the downstroke "May the negative be transformed" and on the upstroke "May the positive manifest." Do this with each candle and each oil before placing the candle in its holder in the center of the altar table.

Dressing the Table: Now it is time to use the sixteen objects you removed earlier from the cleansing tea (stones, feathers, coins, and seashells).

For the North Altar: Place the four pieces of money at the four cardinal points around the candle.

Now you may place any other objects you have for the North altar wherever you please. Each object should be dipped in the cleansing tea (or sprayed), dried, and then placed. This procedure is to be followed for each altar.

In the North I recommend a pine cone, bone, or animal horn, a quartz crystal or white stone, a piece of fur, and a bowl of grain.

For the East Altar: Place the four dried feathers at the four cardinal points around the candle. Then place the other objects. I recommend a dried leaf, an amethyst crystal, a stick of incense, and a bowl of cotton balls.

For the South Altar: Place the four stones at the four cardinal points around the candle. Now place the other objects. I recommend a piece of tree bark, a bloodstone, a glass of pomegranate juice, and a bowl of dried red peppers.

For the West Altar: Place the four seashells at the four cardinal points around the candle. Now place the other objects. I recommend a piece of dried seaweed, a piece of turquoise, mother-of-

pearl, or rose quartz, a bowl of seawater, saltwater, or tap water colored blue, and a piece of driftwood.

Dressing It Up: You may also use images of places, creatures, and actions that belong to each direction. For example:

North: Pictures of mountains, horned four-legged creatures, or an old woman sitting quietly.

East: Pictures of a sunrise, birds in flight, or a little girl at play.

South: Pictures of a volcano erupting, a flaming dragon, or a couple making love.

West: Pictures of a seascape with moonlight, a whale, or a pregnant woman.

The intent is to fill each altar with embodiments of its directional attributes.

When you have finished dressing the altars, go to the bathroom and prepare your ritual bath.

The Ritual Bath

Draw a tub of warm water, or take a shower. Scrub your head and body vigorously with a mixture of salt, honey, and your favorite perfume. After you bathe or shower and scrub, rinse your body clean. Take the remainder of your cleansing tea and pour it over your head. Allow the tea to saturate your head, drip down your spine, chest, belly, pubis, legs, arms, hands, and feet.

If the building of these altars is a group venture, the four people should bathe together, scrubbing each other, and pouring the tea over each other's bodies.

Dry off and rest for a little while. If the ritual room is sufficiently heated, the next part of the ritual should be done naked. If it is too cold for that, then dress for optimum health and comfort.

Invocation to the Directions

Center: Stand in the center of the room. Invoke the power of the trickster. Visualize yourself as the spark of all beginnings. Ask for the power to truly change your life in the coming year.

North: Move from the center to the North. Stand before the North altar and invoke the powers of the North and the Northern ancestors (the Europeans and/or whatever people inhabit the land north of where you are). Ask for the power of manifestation and the preservation of the Earth in the coming year. Return to the center.

East: Move from the center to the East. Stand before the East altar and invoke the powers of the East and the Eastern ancestors. Ask for inspiration and the peaceful use of technology in the coming year. Return to the center.

South: Move from the center to the South. Stand before the South altar and invoke the powers of the South and the Southern ancestors. Ask for personal courage, for the healing of sexually transmitted disease, the end of sexual abuse, and the cooling of international temperaments in the coming year. Return to the center.

West: Move from the center to the West. Stand before the West altar and invoke the powers of the West and the Western ancestors. Ask for a beautiful interior life, for sweet dreams and loving family. Ask for the health and protection of women and children, and for better understanding between women and men in the coming year. Return to the center.

If this ritual is a group effort, the invocation to the directions can be shared by five people. Choose one person to hold the center. The other four people will stand around her facing their respective directions, each moving in turn to her direction and remaining there until all the directions have been invoked. At the end of the invocation, everyone will return to the center.

If it is your intention to perform other Winter rituals in this room, leave the invocations intact. To extinguish the candles simply pinch the flames with moistened fingers. Do not blow the candles out. Be mindful that anything that occurs in this room occurs in ritual space and carries intentional power.

For the next two days you will want to sit quietly in the center of this room. I recommend fifteen minutes in the morning or just before you go to bed at night. There is no need to struggle for anything. Simply sit. If any impressions, memories, thoughts, or feelings come to you, simply jot them down. They may be helpful later. But right now, simply sit down and allow yourself to be influenced by the energy of the directions you have invoked. If you like, you may go to sleep here and dream.

Ritual of the Cleansing Fire

For this ritual you will need:

1. the four stones from your South altar
2. a notebook or tablet
3. a lead pencil
4. an eraser
5. a metal container (cast-iron pot, stainless-steel bowl, or aluminum baking pan)
6. a combustible liquid (such as lighter fluid, fingernail polish remover, or rubbing alcohol)
7. a box of matches
8. your bathtub or a large water bucket

Reaffirm your invocation to the South. Ask specifically for the courage to face yourself and the strength to transform yourself. Ask for the passion to release the old with enthusiasm. Relight the South candle.

Sit in the center of your ritual room with your notebook and pencil in hand. Review the past twelve months of your life. Think of all the regrets, frustrations, failures, and injustices that you have endured. Think of how the world's problems have affected you as a child of the Earth. Anything that reads as a setback, sorrow, or weight on your shoulders should be listed on these pages. Be sure you have privacy so that you can talk honestly with yourself. If this room is being shared, an oath of privacy must be taken by each person. It will not do to hold back for fear that your space-mate will read something painful or insulting.

Do not reread what you have written. Now vigorously erase all that you have written. Don't brush the eraser gum off the page.

Take your metal container, the fluid, and the matches into your bathroom. If you are using a bucket, place the container in the bucket, and the bucket in the bathtub. Put the four stones from the South altar in the bottom of the metal container; crumple the erased pages and put them on top of the stones. Now sprinkle them with a small amount of fluid. Put enough water in the tub or bucket to reach the rim of your metal container but not flow into it. The main point is fire safety.

Precautions

Put the fluid away. Be sure none has dripped anywhere. Wash your hands. Pin your hair back if it is long. Get the shower curtain, towels, bath oils, and so on out of the way.

Step back. We are playing with *Fire* here—the radical transformer—and proper respect is due.

Strike a match and say, "By the power of the flame, be ye no more," and throw the match in the metal container. Watch your past problems burn, burn, burn. Truly divorce yourself emotionally from the burning matter. Be pleased that it's going up in flames. In fact, laugh.

When the papers have burned, turn the water on in the bathtub until the water flows over into the container. Then turn it off. Remove the four stones from the container. Pour the water and ashes into the toilet and flush it. Return the four stones to the South altar.

Now add salt and hot water to the water in your tub, take a refreshing bath, and relax.

A Thankful Thought

Performing rituals such as the one above can have an immediate positive effect. We wake up the next morning feeling ourselves in control, sometimes, even if the negative condition is still present around us. But our skin-sense tells us that the naysayers at work will be transferred soon, the money is coming, our nerves are spared, and future success is assured.

December 21–28, Ritual for Yemaya-Olokun

Here I make two assumptions. I assume that most people get a Christmas vacation (to vacate means to empty out), and that most of you will have an obligatory "traditional" Christmas gathering to attend. My Pan-Africanist Black, Islamic, Jewish, and Buddhist sisters will please ignore these assumptions.

I have placed this ritual within the context of a seven-day period. You may choose to do this particular ritual any day between December 21 and 31, if you like.

Pan-Africanists may choose an appropriate day within Kwanzaa week to perform it instead of, or in addition to, the requirements of that holiday. What is important is that the days before this ritual should be introspective.

For this ritual you will need:

1. a recording of sounds of the Ocean
2. clothing that reflects the colors of the Sea
3. objects from the Sea and/or those associated with the qualities of the Sea (seashells, coral, silver objects, Moonshapes, and mirrors)
4. a seven-day deep-blue candle in a glass
5. a seven-day green candle in a glass
6. a large bowl with blue water in it
7. blessed anointing oil (I recommend Meditation or Sweet Dreams oil)
8. small musical instruments
9. seven dimes
10. a folk or fairy tale about Merpeople or Ocean creatures
11. songs and food to share
12. smudge in a seashell
13. a silver bell

The West Altar: The West altar should be well dressed for this ritual. I recommend a color scheme of satiny deep blue, luminescent silver, and seaweed green. If you can secure a piece of cloth with an Ocean motif, lay it on the floor in front of the altar. This is the altar mat where people will place their objects and offerings. Place the bowl of blue water in the center of the altar mat.

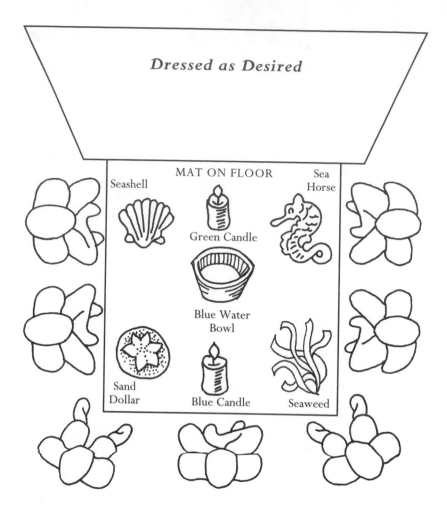

Put the deep-blue candle in the South next to the bowl; and put the green candle North of the bowl. Begin the Ocean tape.

Entry: As the participants (hereafter referred to as family) enter the room, place ritual objects on the altar mat. Choose a comfortable place to sit. (I recommend pillows on the floor with room to lie down.) Listen to the sounds of the Ocean and be quiet.

Smudge: The *oldest woman* in the house (or She Who Has the Most Children) should mix a smudge of sage, rosemary, hyssop, and lemon verbena and smudge the altars and the people. As she does this, moving West, North, East, and South, the *youngest woman* in the house (or She Who Has No Children) should follow her, ringing a silver bell.

Directions: If you have left the directions intact from our earlier rituals, simply reaffirm them. If your personal wisdom advises, invoke the directions full force. In either case you will want to begin in the West for this ritual and then move North, East, and South, asking for the transformative power in each. The family stands and faces each direction as it is invoked.

Deep-Sea Chant: Hand-in-hand with eyes closed, the family takes seven slow deep breaths, breathing in the sound and feel of the Ocean's depth. Now family members call out the names of Sea deities (Godesses and Gods) and chant these names. Play with the names, stretch the vowels, hammer the consonants, allow them to crescendo and decrescendo into a cacophony of sound. Return to silence. Listen to the sounds of the Ocean. Melt down into your seats, lie down on the floor, relax in Yemaya's arms.

Guided Visualization: This visualization should be spoken by one who has a soothing voice. The sounds of the Ocean are the background music; occasionally the tinkle of the maiden's silver bell is heard. Light the blue candle.

The visualization should take the family back to Mother's womb, to the depths of the Ocean. It should speak to the creative and regenerative powers of Mother's womb and Father's seed. Each member is encouraged to re-create herself, to compose a new person for the New Year.

This visualization should be delivered impromptu. Reading from a prepared script would destroy the virginity of it.

The speaker should visually walk into the Ocean, experience devolution and union with Her other life-forms, return to a single cell, and re-create herself. If you are the speaker, speak the directives that will seduce others into similar feelings as you are experiencing this re-creation. In this way the speaker will remain part of the flow. Let your own words come through as you speak.

The Recovery: As the visualization ends, the family will open their eyes and sit up. Now it is time to share the experiences on the Ocean's bottom. Members will volunteer to share their stories. Anyone who wishes to remain silent may do so. Invite family members to choose a name or title for themselves that bespeaks their experience below: Seaweed Woman, Green Dolphin Queen, Aqua Marine, for example.

Now pass the anointing oil around the circle. Each person should anoint her third eye (between the eyebrows), her heart (between the breasts), and her navel while pronouncing the name she has acquired. Some will want to identify themselves, using the name before the altar throughout the coming year. If the name is that of a sea creature, it may be used as a dream totem. Ask your personal wisdom if this totem is your dream companion for the year.

*Make Mary:** After the anointing, members may pick up their small instruments and begin to create a "makeshift orchestra." Begin with a steady drumbeat, something soft and comforting. Let instruments join in at will. Build the music up. Get up and move your body. Swim through the space; flip, flop, and dive through the air. Each person should stop playing and dancing at will. Decrease the music and the movement until there is only the sound of the drum, the silver bell, and the Ocean in the background.

* The Christian Mary, or Star of the Sea.

The Mother of Secrets: Each person will bring out the seven dimes. Whisper your hopes, dreams, aspirations to the seven dimes. Take your time. Be clear. When you are ready, go to the bowl of blue water. Say "All powerful, all healing, most beautiful Mother, give birth," and drop the dimes in the Ocean.

Each person will dip her hands in the water, just enough to carry a wet hand over to her ritual object on the altar mat. Sprinkle your ritual object with Ocean water, pick it up, and return to your seat.

At this point a woman should deliver an Oriki (praise-poem) in honor of the Ocean. A few words will do. Simply share a personal story about the beauty and power of the Ocean or confess how much you love Her, thank Her for Her undying dance, Her endless nurturing.

Close the Directions: Lightly or firmly dismiss the directions South, East, North, and West. Share food, conversation, and song. Read a folktale. Play like children.

Rituals for the New Year

For this ritual you will need:

1. your personal power oil
2. one yard of white cloth
3. a needle with black thread in it
4. a red felt-tipped pen
5. a handful of the herb thyme
6. your favorite grain or seed
7. pushpins or staple gun

Measure the width of the doorway to your ritual room. Then cut a piece of white cloth that wide and about twelve inches long.

With the needle and thread make a small hem in one side of the cloth. Large stitches will do, as we wish to see the black thread moving through the white cloth. At the other end of the cloth, tear it into twelve strips about six inches up the length of the cloth. With your red pen write the months of the year on each strip: January, February, and so on through December.

Now mix your thyme with your grain or seed. Say a prayer asking for good fortune and fulfillment, and breathe on the mixture. Put a pinch of it into the end of the monthly strips, and tie each of the strips. Now you have twelve knots of herbs hanging from a common banner. Please make sure the month name shows on each strip. Using pushpins or a staple gun, attach this banner to the doorway of your ritual room. You may want to anoint the banner with your personal power oil.

Put the leftover herb mixture in a metal container and place it on your East altar.

New Year Dream Chart

Your New Year Dream chart is simply a graphic representation of your intentions for the coming year. It is designed to help clarify your intentions, provide a timetable, and serve as a gentle reminder. This chart is your friend, not your slave driver. After you have drawn the chart, post it where it is visible in the course of a normal day. Refer to it throughout the year. At year's end put an *X* next to the things you didn't accomplish and a check mark next to things achieved. *Assess your dream-fulfillment quotient, consider the influence of the trickster, and dream again.*

The sample chart shown here is *a* way, not *the* way to set up a New Year Dream chart. You should design one that suits your lifestyle. If you have a paid vacation every summer, your chart will be different from mine. If I find a free weekend in any year I count it as a blessing.

The important thing is to be inspired and practical at the same time; and leave a few loopholes that the trickster can play in.

Ring in the New Year

In preparation for this ritual you will need a new garment—a comfortable gown, a big shirt, or whatever apparel will give you maximum comfort. Place the garment on the East altar (folded or hanging above). Be sure you have *the container of herbs from making the banner* on the altar, along with matches and your personal oil.

Outside the ritual room you will place an old rag on the floor. Come to the door of the ritual room dressed in raggedy clothes. By raggedy I mean the dress you always seem to be wearing during a bad argument, the purse you tend to carry when you're broke, and the shoes that led your feet to trouble all last year.

If this is a group ritual, have a ripping party. Rip the old clothes off yourself or each other with vigor and great relief. You may cuss and scream or laugh hysterically if you choose. Just make sure the emotion displayed truly expresses the way you've felt about the past year. Kick these ripped rags behind you and wipe your feet on the old floor rag. *As you pass through the doorway raise your palms up.* Be sure that your head and hands are brushed by the herb packets of your door banner. Walk immediately to the East altar.

Invoke the East: As the gateway to attainment, the brilliance of the rising Sun, light the East candle. Declare with as much conviction as possible that you are ready to receive your greatest good every month of the coming year. Light the container of herbs and smudge your New Year garment. Be sure to smoke it inside and out. Then saturate the cotton balls (placed there earlier) with your personal oil and anoint the top of your head, third eye, heart, pubis, palm of each hand, and soles of both feet. In a group, anoint each other, blessing

New Year Dream Chart

	January	February	March	April
Spiritual Development	Ritual for Elegba	St. Valentine ritual	Spring Equinox	Earth Day ritual
Health & Fitness	Diet & exercise	Diet & exercise	Spring tonic	
Career & Finances	Assess my savings	Create Spring show	Perform Spring show →	
Domestic & Family	Weatherproof windows	Fertilize the garden	Spring cleaning	
Political Activism	MLKing birthday	Black History Month	International Women's Day	Earth Day demonstration
Travel & Personal	Learn to sing →			

each place. Say what you feel. Sincerity is more important than formality in this ritual. Now dress in your New Year garment. Play, eat, sing, dance—rejoice that you have ritually set the stage for a beautiful year.

May	June	July	August	September ...
		Summer Solstice		
	Exercise & prepare for Africa ⟶			Take swimming class
Get Africa ticket			Shop for school clothing	School starts
		Find house sitter		
	Juneteenth celebration			
		Go to Africa		

⌣·

While making the New Year Dream chart and the twelve-month door banner, you have been involved in an extrovert meditation.* Perhaps you found it all a bit tedious. But doing the work has caused you to focus, to invest energy in your own future. Whether you realize it or not, you have reevaluated your past and empowered yourself for the future. This is Will-directed prophecy.

If you wish, you may also perform divination for the New Year. You may use Tarot cards, the I Ching, or rune stones.

Divination can be done by concentrating on your aspiration as expressed in the Dream chart. While concentrating on your Will, ask for guidance and direction in fulfilling these aspirations. Always use *operative* questions and statements such as "What must I do? Guide me in right actions. Show me the path I must take to fulfill my aspirations." Then cast the oracle, and record and interpret its message.

As you move into the year, refer to the divination and apply its message to your activities. It is also permissible and advisable to divine again at the equinoxes and solstices, on your birthday and anniversary, as well as at the New and Full Moons.

The point is to create a balance between Will and Law and to chart one's progress through the year. Doing this will assure a fruitful and exciting year in spite of all external circumstances.

---

* An extrovert meditation involves the integration of spiritual contemplation, mental calm, and physical action. The Yoruba word for it is *ebbo*.

Spring

The Daughter of Promise

The Birth of Human Beings

Children will not be wanting at the hand of the Mother, young children will not be wanting at the foot of the banana tree.

The Holy Odu Ogbe Meji

There in the garden stood a creature made from the desire of Moon, composed in the likeness of Sun. There in the garden stood a creature made from the desire of Sun, in the image of Moon. They stood looking at each other, uncertain of who they were and how they came into Being.

Sensing their dilemma, the Serpent opened Its mouth and spat forth a rain of knowledge followed by a shower of love. The two creatures gazed at each other, their hearts pounding in their chests. Slowly the Sun and Moon within them began to stir until they could only embrace and mingle their substances in a dance of delight.

As they danced the banana tree rumbled and produced long yellow fruit. As they danced the Earth shook and produced millet. They danced and all existence multiplied itself. The Divine Twins felt the fertility of the Earth pulse through them and spread from them to the land and back again. And they laughed because it was Spring.

(Original tale, L. Teish, 1988)

Daughter of Promise

Oriki Oshun

Iyalode Oshun. Goddess of the River. Daughter of
Promise. Mother of the Sweet Waters.

It is from Your throbbing Womb that the rhythm of Music
springs. It is from Your bouncing Breasts that Dance is
born.

We hear Your voice in the babbling brook. We see Your
eyes in the Morning Star. At Sunrise we behold You.

We lie among the wildflowers to inhale the scent of Your
skin. Your smile sprinkles us with pollen.

Teardrops of orchid nectar roll sweetly down Your cheeks.
We raise our faces to the heavens, spring rain falls
gently upon us.

In the cool of evening, in the shade of the New Moon,
Your veiled mirror shines. We see Your eyes in the
Evening Star. Then we reach into each other, and
embrace and make love as a tribute to the silhouette
of Your Greatness.

In undulating ripples You move through our bodies . . .
promising . . . promising. The blood in our veins turns
to Moonlight, flowing.

Our hearts burst open like new flower blossoms. Sweating
perfume and honey we come to You amidst laughter
and tears of joy.

You are the beauty that makes life worth living.
You are the power that renews.

You are the passion to pursue the promise,

Love,

    Love,

        Love.

L. Teish, for Oshun Ibukole, Spring 1987

The Spring Maiden

It begins in Spring. The seeds that have been lying peacefully in the Earth during Winter's dormancy begin to push their way through the casing. Clouds give forth their blessing in the form of rain. The gentle warm rays of the Sun provide quickening, urging barren trees to turn green with baby blossoms. Their fragrance perfumes the air.

We inhale this scent and the waters of our bodies begin to bubble. Like newborn babies we giggle and preen. We dance within ourselves; our joy is hard to suppress.

We long for recreation. Perhaps it begins with a tune. A little finger-popping, head-snapping, hip-shaking tune. Take a plunge in blue water, or a bath in the warmth of a bright yellow Sun. Then the Spring waters begin to well up in us. We go in search of flowers, for a colorful hat.

Imagining that a walk in the park is what we're after, we stop in a record shop or run through the local florist. It satisfies the urge—temporarily—but the desire to reach out and touch the hand of another is what we're really after. Love is what we are seeking. Love in all its forms: love of Life, love of Earth, love of self, friend, and mate.

Oshun, the Daughter of Promise, intoxicates us with Her honey; we are caught in Her web. She pulls us toward the water, the flowers, the warmth of the Sun. Our bodies want to press close together, then pull away. We are caught in Her tease. She teases us into a game of Re-Creation. And all of us—plant, animal, and human—respond to the bubbling fertility of Earth, the hunger for Birth.

In European mythology this Goddess is identified as the spring maiden, the youngest aspect of the Feminine Trinity—Maiden, Mother, and Crone. She has been revered since the advent of agriculture some twelve thousand years ago. She is the archetype for the renewal of the Earth and may be symbolized in a number of ways.

She is the flow of sweet water (river, rain, etc.). The rain brought fertility to the plant and animal life of the forest where humans first gathered edible plants and hunted animals for their hides.

She is the productivity of the fields. With the invention of irrigation the wild lands became controllable farms. River water was brought inland to nurture the Earth, thereby producing food in abundance. Crop surpluses could be used to barter for goods and create wealth, and seeds could be stored for seasonal planting. Through Her, financial security was born.

And just as She stimulated the growth of flowers, the genitalia of the plants, She also came to represent human sexual desire and the impulse to create.

Our ancestors observed the cycles of nature. They saw the Earth's power emerge, increase, flourish, and decline. This observation they mythologized. They created stories to explain the changing seasons. Their tales are full of both mischievous and marvelous characters.

They created these stories to explain Nature to themselves. We have inherited these stories and their wisdom. By understanding early human comprehension of Nature we can trace the thoughts and feelings that evolved into culture. We can change our behavior in relation to Nature, thereby changing our culture. We can create a culture that is based on Nature, grounded in a full understanding of our present needs. These tales may serve as record and guidelines for the cocreators of our futures.

This Goddess has many names. In Egypt She was known as *Hathor,* the Winged Cow of Creation. The Greeks called Her *Aphrodite,* the "titillator." In India She is the beautiful and prosperous *Laksmi.* She is *Indara* of Indonesia and the ever-renewing *Haumea* of the Hawaiian Islands. In the Peruvian Andes She is *Cocomama,* the matron of the coca plant and women's sexuality. In the Yucatan She is *Ix Chel;* among the Apache, *Painted Woman.* In Haiti She is *Erzulie* the "irresistible." She is *Oshun Panchagara,* Queen of the Fertility Fest.

Some of the tales about the Spring Maiden exalt Her as the bringer of abundance, joy, and beauty (Hathor). Others say She gave the world things it never should have had (Pandora). Most of the tales depict Her as generous, promiscuous, and beautiful (Oshun).

Iyalode Oshun

Brass and parrot feathers
on a velvet skin
white cowrie shells
on black buttocks.
Her eyes sparkle in the forest,
like the sun on the River.

Oshun is the Queen of the African diaspora, the Feminine Principle.

The shrine of the Goddess is located in Osh where Her river flourishes. The Royal Palace sits in lush with ancient trees and populated with mysterious sculptures. The musical voices of Her priestesses echo through the grove, "Oore ye ye O, ye ye O." Her shrine is the coolest spot in town.

Like Mawu, She is the moisture that balances the blazing heat of the Sun. She is held in high regard by Nature and human beings alike.

She is Maiden, Mother, and Queen. Yoruba folklore attributes many powers to Her. She has numerous lovers and is known by many praise-names; only a few are given below.

Akuara: Her first and most important role is as the Lady of Destiny. Her husband is Orunmila, the Diviner and Prophet. Together they discern and manifest the fate of the world.

Ibukole: She is the Vulture Goddess, the Messenger of Olorun. She has a privileged relationship with Elegba the Trickster-Magician-Linguist and shares with Him the power to carry messages to Olorun, the Owner of the Sky.

Olomoyoyo: In her aspect as Olomoyoyo She is a fierce Goddess, beautiful but bloody and victorious in war.

Yeye Moro: As Yeye Moro She is a ghost catcher and a comforter of the dead.

Panchagara: She is the personification of the Erotic in Nature. It is she who sits as Queen of the Fertility Fest.

In Brazil and Cuba, African religion merged with Catholicism and the image of the Goddess was greatly affected. In this hemisphere She has been identified with Mary and suffers from the

Madonna-Whore complex. She is referred to as La Puta Santa (the Whore Saint) and envisioned as a prostitute of interracial ancestry. Or She may be known as Yeye Kari (Mother of Kindness) and represented by the statue of the Virgin Mary. These appellations speak more to the cultural and political history of these countries than to the power of the Goddess. For She is a virgin but not in the Catholic sense. She is a virgin in the pagan sense—a woman who belongs to Herself and who is free to interact with whomever She chooses. By identifying Her with Mary, "New World" devotees became ashamed of Her promiscuity in folklore and misunderstood the power of Her intercourse. She has, in many places, simply been reduced to a coquette. But in reality She is Iyalode!

> She is the wisdom of the forest
> She is the wisdom of the River. . .
> She cures with fresh water. . .
> She cures the child. . .
> She feeds the barren woman with honey
> and her body swells up like a juicy palm fruit. . . .[11]

In North Africa and the Middle East the Mother aspect of the Goddess gives birth to a male deity who later becomes the Maiden's lover.* He may be seen as a Sun-King who dies after the harvest; or as a Rain God who is sacrificed because of failing virility.

In matrilineal societies, the deity was naturally a mother-goddess. As the tribe became patriarchal a father-god be-

---

* This deity may be akin to Orungan who chased Yemaya and Elegba, the penis penetrating the Womb of Creation.

came the rule. As the primitive food-gatherers and hunters had made totems of the plants and animals on which they lived, so in agricultural communities the mother-goddess was associated with the earth that bore the crop, and the father-god with the rain that fertilized the soil.[12]

In some places this belief led to the sacrifice of a male child, the King, or an effigy of them.

The relationship between the Maiden-Mother-Queen and Her Son/King has had a profound effect on culture and civilization today. "These birth pangs of civilization—the passage from food-gathering to food-production, from relative peace to chronic war, from primitive communism to private property and slavery, from mother-right to father-right, from magic to religion—made a deep imprint on folklore."[13]

The people offered sacrifices and awaited a good crop. When the crop arrived the security of the group was assured. The realization that this Fertility Principle could be depended upon year after year brought into being a tradition of sacrifice at the appropriate time and a sense of long-range security for the coming generations. An active joy was expressed at planting time, and a great celebration usually followed the harvest.

The connection between the fertility of the crops and that of animals and human beings is a central theme of the rituals. Ancestors are considered "continuous spirit" passing through physical bodies in various life cycles. The discarded bodies are placed in the Earth. She eats them. As the Earth consumes the bodies, they become compost from which new crops will be born and consumed by generations to come. Those generations are the "continuous spirit" in new bodies, the mothers and fathers of the distant future.

81

The dependability of the Principle of Renewal and its connection to human life brought our ancestors a sense of security and joy, but also a sense of responsibility that compelled them to link the two together in ritual and celebrations. The celebration of the fertility of the land and the sexuality of human beings evolved into ritual orgy.

In Rome a ritual indulgence in sensuality and the fruit of the vine, performed in honor of the Greek god of wine (Bacchus), became known as the Bacchanalia. Today the bacchanalian rite has survived patriarchy, technology, and erosphobia in the seasonal celebration known to us as Carnival.

The Principle of Renewal and its celebrations were consumed by the Christian faith; its original symbols are obscured and handed down to us in the holiday known as Easter.

Carnival in New Orleans

Fat Tuesday

Mardi Gras is New Orleans's grand affair of the year. It extends well beyond the two weeks of actual parading. Revelers begin the celebration just after Christmas with a series of dances that are held almost every night until Mardi Gras.

Carnival organizations are secret societies commonly called "krewes." Each krewe has a theme for the parade, which requires long-range planning, specialized costumes, songs, dances, and pageant dramas.

The name Mardi Gras is generally translated as "Fat Tuesday"—the last day before Lent on which good Catholics may eat meat. Tradition has it that the common people cook red beans and rice with big chunks of salt pork, burn the last of the oil in their lamps, and say farewell to meat for the Lenten season.

But the French word *gras* also means good cheer and implies a time of relaxed morals and merrymaking.

Carnival is a European holiday transported to America. In Europe, it had been a celebration of Earth's renewal, the fertility of Spring. Revelers dressed in animal costumes, pelted each other with flowers, drank the fruit of the vine (Bacchus), and paid homage to the Maiden-Mother and Her Sun/Lover.

The earliest recorded Carnival in North America took place in the South in 1704. Between 1718 and 1799 Louisiana's elite society held impressive private parties. Although the Spanish outlawed masquerading as a means of controlling criminals, the French promoted it. By 1824 Carnivals were very popular and eventually were legalized. But Mardi Gras did not become "tradition" until 1827, when it was promoted by a group of students returning from Paris.

Louisiana Carnivals based their characters on local earth-centered themes. The first Carnival floats (1837) related to agriculture. The King and Queen were "de la Fève," named after a large edible bean. Their props were farming tools; and little boys representing the Son of the Goddess pelted people with sacks of flowers.

The Mardi Gras krewes were often dedicated to aspects of the Grain King. In 1857 the Mystick Krewe of Father Comus, the Roman god of joy, was formed. And Rex, the first "King" of Carnival, appeared in 1872. By 1875 Mardi Gras had become a legal holiday. Today the Rex Parade is the pinnacle of this Spring rite.

On the surface Mardi Gras appeared to be simply a time to get drunk and act out. But beneath its powdered face it was a politico-spiritual movement that celebrated ancient folk beliefs and subtly influenced the government of the city. The King of Mardi Gras "has ever since been entitled on that day to issue proclamations which nominally take precedence over the city ordinances."[14]

Most of this celebrating occurred with a backdrop of Black slavery. The Emancipation Proclamation was not issued until 1863. So Black people participated in Carnival behind the scenes as servants, spectators behind the crowd, and torchbearers alongside the parade. It was not until 1910 that Black people formed their own krewe and gave birth to the Zulu Parade.

Who's Zulu?

Mardi Gras was an issue that caused great consternation in my extended family. It was divided between the Catholics (led by my mother) and the African Methodist Episcopal church members (led by my father). The Catholics thought it was important to celebrate Mardi Gras and Lent. The Protestants liked Mardi Gras but thought Lent was idolatry. Further, on the issue of participation in the holiday, my mother and Aunt Marybelle Reed were proud to be handkerchief dancers. My father felt that it was enough to stand on the side and catch the goodies thrown from the floats, but he was also concerned about the drunkenness and the fighting that inevitably occurred. Moma insisted that with proper protection the children could participate in safe parts of town. Usually this meant that we went to the parade in Algiers and watched the ones in the city of New Orleans on television.

But the real splitting of hairs and gnashing of teeth was reserved for debating the value of the Zulu Parade. It seemed that the entire community had one of two opinions: (1) that it was about time colored folks had something of their own, and (2) that it was a

shame before God for colored folks to make such fools of themselves just to be in the Mardi Gras.

When I was about nine years old my *nanan* (godmother) took
me to the Zulu Parade in New Orleans. There I saw people dressed
up like baby dolls, and a devil took a jab at me with his pitchfork. It
all seemed very chaotic and more than I could process at the time.
So I withdrew my mind from the debate and made myself content
with the candy, jewelry, and toys that other people brought in from
the Mardi Gras.

Twenty years later I attended a Carnival in New Orleans. I was
escorted by a brother, two cousins, and an uncle who were well
armed. Now I recognized the Zulu Parade as the remnants of old
African customs. Certain traditions are so deeply embedded in the
psyche that, like Matter, they cannot be destroyed but simply
change from one form into another. Certain characteristics of the
Zulu Parade bespeak ancestor-reverence practices struggling to
maintain themselves in spite of slavery, poverty, and racism.

The Zulu paint their faces with white chalk. Because of racist
conditioning, pollywogs and the minstrel shows immediately come
to mind. But marking the face with white chalk is a precolonial
spiritual tradition, especially in West Africa, the Motherland of
most Black Americans. The lime chalk (*efun, cascarilla*) is usually
taken from the sediment of the river or the belly of caves. Both are
regarded as important body parts of Mother Earth; and white
chalk on Black faces puts one, chromatically, between the physical
and the spiritual worlds, between the living and the dead.

The raffia skirts the Zulu wear are traditionally used to adorn
the ceremonial hut, to dress the altars of deities, and to cover the
bodies of masqueraders in African ancestral festivals.

William Story was the first king [of the Zulu Parade], wearing a lard-can crown and carrying a banana-stalk scepter. By 1913 progress had reached the point where King Peter Williams wore a starched white suit, an onion stickpin, and carried a loaf of Italian bread as a scepter. In 1914 King Henry rode in a buggy and from that year they grew increasingly ambitious, boasting three floats in 1940, entitled respectively, "The Pink Elephant," on which rode the King and his consort, "Hunting the Pink Elephant," and "Capturing the Pink Elephant."[15]

The banana stalk, the onion stickpin, and the bread all represent the fertility of the Earth because they grow in the body of the Goddess. King Henry, like the great Hannibal, chose the elephant to signify royalty. The elephant is sacred to Obatala. In Africa, it is the elephant, not the lion, who is regarded as king of the jungle. And the threatened extinction of this ancient beast is an omen to us all.

In 1922 the reigning Zulu King reenacted another important African tradition. He rented a yacht—the Royal Barge—and rode it in high style down the New Basin Canal. In Africa, political dignitaries parade downriver to survey their realm and to visit neighboring royalty. Initiations into sacred priesthoods often begin with a ritual at the river; and in Nigeria the great Feminine Force is Oshun, the Goddess of the River. So again we have symbolic intercourse between the Grain King and the Spring Maiden.

The Zulu Kings wore majestic costumes, held court, and dispensed coconuts to the revelers. When a Zulu King died, his body was escorted by a grand marshal, sixteen pallbearers, and a thirteen-piece brass band that played "I'll Be Glad When You're Dead, You Rascal You."

The joyous fertility invoked here has generously spread throughout the nation and the world. The Voudou ceremonies in Congo Square, the songs of Carnival, and the funeral dirges of New Orleans are the ancestors of the great American music form known as jazz. *Egun Re'O.* The ancestors are good.

In addition to Zulu kings and queens, baby dolls and devils, the Black people of New Orleans also paid homage to the ancestors of the land. They created the Krewe of the Black Indians (circa 1920). It is possible that the early participants were of African American and Native American descent. It is estimated that one out of every five Black people in this country has some Native American ancestry. But participation in the Indian parade was based not on ancestry but on affinity with the culture. The Black Indians took Native American names, made splendid costumes, created songs in traditional Native rhythms, and endured the ordeal of becoming chief.

> The Golden Blades were started twenty-five years ago in a saloon. Ben Clark was the first chief and ruled until two years ago, when a younger man took over. Leon Robinson—Chief Happy Peanut—deposed Clark in actual combat, as is the custom. . . . That's the way a chief is created, and that is the way his position is lost.[16]

Again we see a subtext of food (Happy Peanut) and humor and the harvest (golden blades). Still we have a hint of a chief, king, or son who is connected to the land, who shines for a period of time and then is cut down and dies.

Gradually our ancestors changed the "ancient practices." They substituted the slaughter of a fatted calf or goat for the actual sacrifice of the Sun-King. Later, that practice changed into an offering of grain. It became tradition, in some places, to make animal images out of bread dough and place them in the Earth; or to make an image of the Sun-King out of cornstalks or wheat straw and burn it.

The rebirth of the Grain King and his relationship to the Maiden-Mother of fertility has been preserved, however obscured, in the symbolism and traditions of Easter.

Stand Up for Lent

In the seventh grade I went to All Saints School in Algiers, Louisiana. There we were required to attend mass regularly, have catechism every morning, eat fish on Friday, and of course observe all the Catholic holidays.

This school was composed of two classes of kids: the genteel poor who were struggling to "do better," and the *pasabonne*. Louisiana still had remnants of a caste system based on skin color. A *pasabonne* was a Black person fair enough to pass for white. Sometimes they did; sometimes they didn't. Often these people had businesses of their own and identified with themselves rather than with Black or White. It was common to find someone who was telephone black and French vanilla fair in the same family. The nuns who ran the school were a combination of both.

In my school there was a pasabonne beauty whom I will call
Dimples DuPree. She was vanilla with gray eyes and sandy red

hair. She was considered the prettiest girl in school. And she had taken up with Juan Birdcage, who was "Indian tan" with raven-black hair and changeable brown to green eyes. *

The crème, caramel, and dark chocolate beauties and beaux of the school were interested in these two; but tradition dictated that they would marry each other or become a nun and a priest.

One day Sister Mary Ann Abstencia announced to the class that Lent was just around the corner and that we'd all better start thinking about what we would give up for the Holy Season. She added that it should be something precious, something you really loved.

For days people discussed what they would give up. They decided, argued with each other, and changed their minds. Finally the morning came when Sister Abstencia asked each student to stand up and announce what he or she would be giving up for Lent.

Some gave up their favorite TV program; some gave up pig lips and potato chips. Rosy Pelonegro gave up twisting her hair, and Johnny Fishbone said he gave up, period. Dimples DuPree stood up and proudly announced that she would give up being the prettiest girl in school. She promised not to wear pretty clothes for at least forty days. After her announcement throats cleared, eyes rolled, and people wiggled in their seats. Sister Mary Abstencia lowered her eyes and slapped the ruler on the desk several times. The room got quiet.

Now it was Juan Birdcage's turn to speak. He stood up, folded his hands in front of him, and announced that he was

---

* Not their real names.

89

giving up Dimples DuPree for Lent. He sat down. The class broke out in thunderous laughter—the loud, sharp, crucifying kind that only junior high school kids can deliver. Sister Mary Absten-cia lifted her chin, opened her eyes wide, and banged on the desk until there was silence. Dimples DuPree flushed pink, crimson, and purple.

We all teased her; we called her names for forty days. When asked, Juan Birdcage said he gave her up because Sister said to give up something precious. But he always added that it had been his mother and father's idea. When Lent ended they did not re-sume eating lunch together.

(An original tale)

Another Mother's Son

"Like Horus and Osiris, . . . Jesus too is still the child of a divine Mother. He is in fact the child of the Goddess and, like her earlier divine children, symbolizes the regeneration of nature by his resur-rection every spring at Easter."[17]

For the Christian church—both Catholic and Protestant—Easter is the main calendar event. It celebrates the resurrection of Jesus the Christ, three days after his crucifixion.

Easter is a "movable feast." It always occurs on the first Sunday after the Full Moon following the Spring Equinox (March 21). Once Easter is established, all other movable feasts are placed and the year is set in order.

Easter takes its name from the Saxon fertility Goddess Eostre-Oshtara, who is, by extension, associated with Astarte and Hathor.

And Jesus, the Lamb of God, is the Son of the Maiden Mother

Mary. His life echoes that of the Grain King. Both are born of woman; both are sacrificed for the good of the people; and both are renewed (resurrected) in Spring.

But the Christian Spring festival was not called Easter until the Middle Ages.[18] Many Christian holidays are built on earlier Middle Eastern and Indo-European celebrations.

Joe Worker's Day

In New Orleans a mid-Lent respite from austerity was found in the celebration of St. Joseph's Day (March 19). St. Joseph was a humble and hardworking man whose folk life was emulated by common people, especially Italians and Blacks. The holiday was one of conspicuous display and sharing. Celebrants set a large statue of St. Joseph on the dining table and placed before him several kinds of bread, an abundance of seafood, and various desserts. Poor neighbors and orphans were invited to eat; and money offerings and prayers were left at the foot of the saint in hopes that "St. Joe the worker" would get to work on the petitioner's problem. Bread, lucky beans, and bay leaf were given out. Some people displayed their Carnival costumes on this occasion. But at the stroke of midnight all the feasting stopped and the austerity of Lent continued. If, after three days, St. Joe had not granted the petition, his image was taken out of the house and stood on its head until he started "working."

We did not set the table for St. Joe in my neighborhood. But we regarded him as *the* example of a good man, and people looking for employment or seeking good marriages carried a card of him in their pockets.

The Rabbit and the Egg

During the Easter season we have a bunny rabbit running around in a flowered bonnet, delivering brightly colored chicken eggs.

The Cosmogenetic Egg

Images of Creation

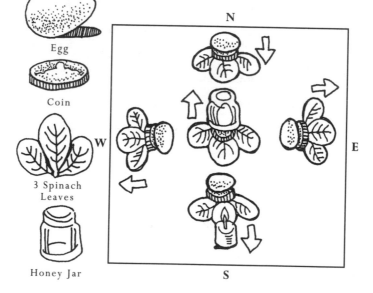

First Rain of May

Egg

Coin

3 Spinach Leaves

Honey Jar

N

W

E

S

The reproductive habits of the rabbit and its connection to pregnancy are well known. This particular rabbit is the Goddess's Moonhare.

The Easter bonnet covered in flowers celebrates the astrological season Aries (March 21–April 20), the first of the Fire Trinity and ruler of the head.

The Egg is a cosmogenetic symbol. People all over the world associate it with potency and birth.

These three symbols clearly show a relationship to earlier ideas of fertility.

A World of Spring

The folklore of indigenous people has added some wonderful aspects to the celebration of Spring.

Palm Sunday (circa A.D. 10) celebrates the palm tree. This tree is a tropical favorite and is regarded as sacred by many people of the world. This is so because of its beauty, abundance, and utility. One folktale about it comes from Brazil.

The Good Tree of Providence

"Long ago, a South American Indian tribe suffered from a drought. They prayed for relief, but in vain. Finally only three Indians remained: a man, his wife, and their child. They left in search of a new home, traveling during the night. The next day they took refuge from the hot sun under the shade of a palm tree. The parents were so exhausted that they fell asleep.

"The little boy, who remained awake, was afraid. He prayed to the god *Tupan* for help. Suddenly he heard a voice. Looking up, he saw an Indian woman in the top of the palm tree. She introduced herself as *Carnauba* and said she would help him. She explained that she and her people had perished from drought many years ago. After her death, the moon had changed her into a palm tree so that she could save the stricken. She told the boy to do the following things: cut open her trunk and drink the sap; eat the fruits of her tree; cook the roots and use them as medicine; dry the leaves and beat them to obtain wax for candles; weave useful articles from the straw that remained.

"In exchange, she asked the boy to plant the nuts from her tree so that new trees would grow. Then she told him to use the lumber from the trunk to build a hut. The boy did all these things.

"Some years later, palm trees grew where the desert once had been. The young Indian, now a man, said good-bye to his parents and set forth to carry the coconuts of the 'good tree of Providence,' as the natives of Brazil call it today, to Indians everywhere."[19]

There are a number of little rituals that are performed with the palm tree:

1. In France, the graves of relatives are decorated with blessed palm leaves.
2. In Puerto Rico, palm leaves are woven into crosses, which are hung in the house for protection and abundance.
3. In Belgium, pieces of blessed palm are placed in the fields to assure a good harvest.
4. In Cuba, family members sweep each other with blessed palm branches to ward off evil spirits.

5. In New Orleans, palmetto palms are planted near a
   pond on one's property to assure health, luck, and
   love.

Palm nuts are used to divine the will of the Gods in West
Africa, and palm oil is used in a variety of sacred ways. Think about
it. How many ways do you use palm products?

Like New Orleans, Brazil and the Caribbean Islands have Carnivals with fertility motifs from European, African, and Native
American cultures. And each culture has ways of remembering its
relationship to the Goddess. This is clearly exemplified in an Ar-
gentine rite.

The *tincunac* ceremony is celebrated on Thursday before
Ash Wednesday. Two groups of women, mothers on one
side and godmothers on the other, form lines on each side
of an arch of willow branches decorated with flowers, fruit,
cheese, sweets, and tiny lanterns. The two groups meet
under the arch and pass a symbolic child, usually made of
candy, from one to another as they touch each other's fore
heads. This sacred ceremony unites the women in a tie that
only death can part. Afterward, rockets are shot off, starch
is thrown and the feasting and dancing begin.

On Sunday, Carnival reaches its climax. The women,
wearing wide ruffled skirts, colorful ponchos, and white
hats, transform their faces with starch and water. After
lunch, everyone washes and returns with a fresh copy of
starch and confetti. Singing folksongs, the people ride on
horseback to the house where they are to dance in honor of

Pukally, the spirit of Carnival. Dancing is interspersed with horseplay as Carnival finally ends. Pukally, a rag doll dressed in native costumes, is buried while the woman playing the part of his widow sobs and others beat drums and sing Carnival songs. Each participant throws a shovelful of dirt into the freshly dug grave as all sing:

¡Ya se ha muerto el carnaval!
Ya lo llevan a enterrar;
Echenle poquita tierra
Que se vuelva a levantar.
(Carnival is dead now!
They are burying him;
Throw just a little dirt in
So he can rise again).[20]

The Spring Rituals

Grounds Blessing

Preparing the Earth for Spring Planting

For this ritual you will need the following things:

1. four winter grains
2. a bottle of tempered water (Ocean and River mixed)
3. one cup of red wine; one cup of white wine (or use sparkling grape and pomegranate juice)
4. a tuber cut into many pieces (potato, yam, or taro root)
5. nuts and berries (walnuts/strawberries/chestnuts/blueberries, etc.)
6. a small jar of honey
7. a feather from a domestic fowl (hen/goose/guinea)
8. a small whole fish (a holy mackerel)
9. a handful of coins (pennies, dimes)
10. a white candle (taper)
11. matches and a wind guard

This ritual is a modified composite. It contains many of the elements of grounds blessings as performed in the African diaspora and other eco-centric traditions. It has been modified to eliminate ritual acts that are restricted or discomforting to the laity; but the power invoked by those acts is represented symbolically and honored spiritually. In this ritual we substitute red wine and fowl feathers for the traditional animal sacrifice.

Although this ritual can be performed by an individual, I am assuming that it will be done by a group. Those of you who do not have outdoor gardens may use planter boxes and become apartment farmers; or you may use a flowerpot to perform the ritual and leave it as an offering in your neighborhood park.

Clear the garden of last season's waste, compost it, turn the soil, and water it.

Family members should gather four winter grains from the kitchen cabinets. I am assuming that you have eaten oats, wheat, rice, barley, and so on during the cold season. It is good to take the last of these supplies. This represents the end of the cold season. Of course, if you keep your cabinet full of grains year-round, simply take a handful and thank the grain for having sustained you through the winter. Put the grain in small bags, bowls, or other convenient containers. Gather it up along with the other ingredients.

A wind guard is any device that allows a candle to sit in the earth without being disturbed by the wind. You can make a dirt mound with a deep center; you can remove the top and bottom from fruit juice cans or make cylinders of aluminum foil to place around the candle at ritual's end.

This ritual can be effectively done three days before or three days after the Equinox. To receive the maximum benefit of the

Earth's balancing energy, however, I recommend beginning the ritual at high noon on the Equinox. Whichever day it is performed, it should be finished before sundown, so that the garden and the family will receive full benefit from the Sun and the Moon.

Take all the ingredients to the garden. Dig a hole four inches deep or deeper. Family members should stand in a circle, barefoot, around the hole. Clasp hands and take nine slow, deep breaths. Feel the warmth of the Sun on your face and the coolness of the Earth beneath your feet.

Invocation to the Directions

The East: Family members should all face the East. A selected person will lead the invocation by verbally creating visions of the power of Seed. Here we describe the potential of Seed lying quietly in the dark womb of the Earth. Seed contains the ancestral memory of its genus and species. Describe various seeds: small ones, encased ones, bulbs, and eyes. Feel the seed receiving water, being caressed by the nurturing soil. See the seed bursting open. Blessed be the power of the Seed.

The South: Family members should all face the South. A selected person invokes the power of Stalk. Here we see the stalk bursting forth from the seed, pushing its way through the soil, struggling, and breaking ground to feel the clear rays of the first sunlight. As the stalk stretches skyward it also sends its roots deeper into the Earth. The stalk develops strength. Blessed be the power of Stalk.

The West: Family members should all face the West. A selected person invokes the power of Flower. Here we see the flower's bud at the end of the stalk. Flower begins to open, unfolding, displaying itself. Flower is sensuous, and vain. Flower drips nectar, flashes bright colors, fills the air with scent. Flower is beautiful. Blessed be the power of Flower.

The North: Family members should all face the North. A selected person invokes the power of Fruit. Now we see Fruit in the great variety of things that Earth gives us to eat. We see squash and corn, lettuce and tomatoes, bananas and oranges. Fruit is the reward of labor and a medicine to those who consume it. Fruit is tasty and abundant. And most important, fruit contains the seed of future possibility. Fruit is fulfillment. Blessed be Fruit. Return to the center.

Respect for the Ancestors

At this point we want to pay homage to our ancestors. For this ritual we will call the names of blood relatives who lived reasonable lives and died under relatively decent circumstances. We will also call the names of affinity spirits: those who maintain an important relationship to you but are not blood kin (your favorite teacher); and those whose lifework has contributed to the advancement of the Earth (your favorite ecologist). They are all people who have stepped to the other side of the veil of life.

Pouring Libation: Take the tempered water in hand. Expose it briefly to the four directions. Pour water four times into the hole:

1. In appreciation for your own life.
2. In appreciation for the work of those who have gone before.
3. In appreciation for those who will return.
4. To ask that the bitter and the sweet of life be balanced.

Now call off the names of your ancestors (as defined above). After each name say, "Love and respect to you." When you have run out of names say, "Love and respect to all those whose names I do not know." One person may pour for the group.

Praise-Singing the Earth: Now the family members should sing the praises of the Earth. Begin by thanking the Earth for all She has given us. Thank Her for the beauty of Her precious stones, Her delicious water, and Her wonderful flowers. Thank Her for sustaining plant, animal, and human life. Apologize on behalf of those who have raped and poisoned Her. Then renew your commitment to Her healing and that of Her children. Be sincere. Sing songs in praise of the Earth.

Winter's Grain: Take a handful of each grain. Expose it briefly to the four directions. Thank the grain for sustaining you through the Winter. Breathe on the grain. Toss it into the hole. Each person does this.

The Tuber: Each person takes a piece of the potato, yam, or taro root and exposes it briefly to the four directions. Thank the Earth for providing tubers and thank our ancestors for finding them. Place the pieces of tuber in the middle of the bed of grain.

Nuts and Berries: Each person exposes the nuts and berries to the four directions. Remember our ancestors' transition from food gathering to food growing. Take a moment to appreciate the difficulties in gathering and the work involved in farming. Thank the ancestors for their intelligence and the Earth for Her support.

The Offerings: The following offerings should be made by two people on behalf of the group. One will represent the Moon, the Feminine Principle in Nature. The other will represent the Sun, the Masculine Principle in Nature. Typically these would be an old woman and a young man. But, in reality, these positions should be appointed according to the composition of your group. What is essential is that these two people maintain their roles through the next steps of the ritual.

The Red Wine: Mother Moon will expose the red wine to the four directions. It represents the power of woman's menstrual blood and its role in the creation of new life. Pour four drops of red wine into the hole.

The White Wine: Sun-Father will expose the white wine to the four directions. It represents the power of man's seminal fluid and its role in the creation of new life. Pour four drops of white wine into the hole.

Fish and Fowl: Moon-Mother will touch the fowl feather to the Earth at her feet and thank Sun-Father for his life-quickening rays. Then she will commit the feather to the hole.

Sun-Father will lift the small fish up to the sky and thank Mother Ocean for all Her wondrous gifts. Then he will commit the fish to the hole.

The Honey: The honey should be exposed to the four directions. Each person pours a little honey and asks that her and his life be sweetened, that the family's life be sweetened, that Heaven and Earth be sweetened.

The Coins: Each family member takes a handful of coins and exposes them to the four directions. Invoke the Principle of Reciprocity. Remember that all wealth comes from the Earth, that barter was the first form of business, and that all must be returned to the Earth. Ask the Earth to accept your gift and to give an abundant crop. Promise to share your wealth with others. Toss the coins in the hole.

Closing the Hole: All the family members should use their hands to rake the dirt back into the hole. You may want to make a mound with a deep hole in the center, which can serve as a wind guard for your candle. Otherwise close the hole firmly. Place a white candle in the center of the mound/circle. If you are using a wind guard, put it in place around the candle. Now give thanks to the Earth, the ancestors, and the four directions. Walk away.

After the candle has burned out, proceed with the planting of your garden. This spot need not be marked in any way and it is all right to walk on it. Next spring you may choose a different spot. You are simply replenishing the Earth in a sacred manner.

Pots and Boxes: If you have performed this ritual using a pot or planter box, you may want to let this one "grow wild" in your apartment. Or you may leave it under a bush or at the foot of a tree in the park or forest. Once you have offered it, leave it alone.

Bath in the First Rain in May

For this ritual you will need:

1. a new bucket, a large plastic jar with lid, and a bowl
2. fifteen large leaves of fresh spinach
3. five fertile eggs
4. a jar of honey
5. your personal oil or perfume
6. one yard of yellow cotton cloth
7. a yellow devotional candle
8. five pieces of money (nickels, quarters, or Susan B. Anthony dollars)

Wash the bucket and the plastic jar with salt water. Rinse thoroughly. Reserve them for this ritual.

On the first day that rain falls in the month of May, place this bucket outside to collect the water. You may place the bucket in your garden, on the roof, or on the porch. Or you can suspend it by a rope out your window. Under ideal circumstances the water would be caught between sunrise and sunset. But catch it when you can.

If pollution would make the rainwater unfit to bathe in, buy a bottle of springwater from your local store. Most rituals of this kind were born before pollution was a problem.

Immediately after catching the water, put it in the jar and mark it "Not for Drinking." Store it in the refrigerator until you are ready to use it.

It will take three days to prepare this mixture for your bath.

First Night

Lay the yellow cloth on the floor in front of your altar or some other private place. Remove the lid from the jar of honey and dip your finger in the honey. Taste the honey (preferably in the presence of a witness). Place the honey jar in the center of the cloth.

The Eggs: Take each egg into your cupped hands. Lift each egg up toward the heavens, visualizing the height of space. Touch each egg to the floor while visualizing the depths of Earth. Then expose each egg to the East, South, West, and North while visualizing an open field, a scorching desert, a tropical forest, and a snowcapped mountain. Ask for the power to Think, Create, Sustain, and Release.

Inhale the air emanating from each egg; then exhale, giving the egg your own breath.

Place one egg in the jar of honey. (If it spills over, all the better.) Then place an egg in each of the four directions on the yellow cloth.

The Candle: Fasten the yellow candle to its holder and place it in front of the South egg.

Sit comfortably before this arrangement and visualize every herb, fruit, flower, or vegetable seed you can remember.

Talk with *Yalode*. Tell the Goddess that you marvel at the talent, power, and beauty contained in every seed, in Spring, in the cells of your body. Allow your power of vision to grow freely. Think of things you would like to be able to do well or better. Especially think of all the things others have tried to discourage you from doing. Conjure up creative things that would be great fun to do. See yourself secure in the knowledge that Her power is within you.

Soon you will feel an amorphous and unreasonable sense of wealth, beauty, and power. When this feeling comes, simply accept it and celebrate it by dipping your little finger in the honey and tasting it. *Do not shift into a "how-to" mode.* Do not argue the practical aspects of your vision now.

When the temptation to plan gets too strong, put the candle out with your fingertips and go to bed.

Second Night

Tonight you will need fifteen large, fresh spinach leaves and five coins.

Center Three Leaves: Take the first three leaves and speak into them your desire to be creative and fruitful in all that you do. Lift the jar of honey and place the leaves in a fan-shaped figure with their tips pointing North (the area of physical manifestation). Place a coin in the center of this arrangement and put the honey jar on top of the coin.

East Three Leaves: Speak into these leaves. Ask for true inspiration. Ask for originality and inventiveness. Place the leaves in a fan-shaped figure pointing East. Put a coin in the center of the fan and place the egg on top of the coin.

South Three Leaves: Speak into these leaves, asking for strong motivation and passionate involvement in your work. Place the leaves in their fan shape, pointing South. Put a coin in its center and place the egg on top of the coin.

West Three Leaves: When you speak into these leaves, address the healing effect that your action will have on yourself, your extended family, and your community. Ask that the fruits of your labor be well received by all who encounter them. Make the fan of leaves pointing West, place the coin in its center, and put the egg on top.

North Three Leaves: Here in the North ask for wisdom. Ask for the patience to live on Nature's schedule. And ask that all your wisest dreams manifest in good time. Make the fan of leaves pointing North, with their tips reaching for the center. Place the coin and put the egg on top.

The Candle: Now relight your yellow candle. Sit before this beautiful arrangement and visualize yourself at work on some important creative project. If methods begin to reveal themselves, *write them down now!*

But most important, see the project finished. See yourself exhibiting, sharing, performing the work of your dreams. You may feel like humming or singing now. Do it.

When your song ends and the feeling of exhilaration decreases, put the candle out and go to bed. (Note: Sometimes these Oshun rituals will spark erotic urges. In this case go to bed, but not to sleep. This energy can be focused on an intimate partner and lo, autoeroticism.)

Third Night

Tonight you will take your bath in the first rain of May.

Begin with the large plastic jar mentioned earlier and the bowl. Be sure that the bowl is clean. Take the egg from the center of the honey jar. Allow the honey to drip into your mixing jar. Take your time. Enjoy watching it drip slowly. Think of it as Oshun juice. Then crack the egg open. Separate the egg white from the yolk. Let the white fall into the bowl. Put the yolk in the jar. Repeat this process with the East, South, West, and North eggs. Take a good look at the yolks in the mixing jar—they are your creative power. Now pour all the honey from the honey jar onto the egg yolks. Add five drops of your personal oil or per-fume, the five coins, and the rainwater from your refrigerator. Now screw the top onto this jar and gently turn the jar from top to bottom to top until the contents are well mixed. Put your spinach leaves in the yellow cloth, pick up your candle, and move to the bathroom.

Preparing Your Bath: Your bathroom should, of course, be clean. If you have a nice incense (I recommend Frangipanni or Come to Me), burn it. Light your yellow candle. It is nice to have a picture of a lake or waterfall on the wall to look at. Get a piece of soothing music or one of those environmental tapes of a flowing stream. Employ every resource at your disposal to create the feeling that you are near a natural body of sweet water.

Fill your bathtub with water at a pleasant temperature. Stand before the tub and invoke the five directions.

Explain to Oshun the steps you have taken to perform this ritual. Recount briefly the way you have felt, the visions you've seen. Remind Her that She is the Daughter of Promise. Remind Her of Her reputation for beauty and generosity. Say that you are the one who loves Her and wishes to do Her work. Then ask that She bless you and shower you in Her abundance.

Get into your tub. Soak, relax, sing, whatever your heart desires. After a few minutes, begin dipping your spinach leaves into the mixture in the jar. As you dip the leaves, place them on the following spots on your body:

1. top of head
2. left temple
3. right temple
4. base of throat
5. back of neck
6. left breast
7. right breast
8. navel
9. pubis
10. left kneecap
11. right kneecap
12. left foot top
13. right foot top
14. left palm
15. right palm

Ask that all parts of you be in agreement on the things that you have asked for. Let your body and your spirit soak in the vital life force of the spinach leaves. Remain this way for as long as is comfortable. Whatever images come up for you should be allowed to do so; but do not struggle to see. Oju Meta, the third eye, is uncovered and it will do all the work, creating vision and integrating the energies of the other body parts.

My personal tendency at this point is to become sleepy; other women in my family feel suddenly "wired" and ready to get to work. Whatever your natural reaction may be, you will know when to take the next step.

Stand up in your tub. Put the yellow cloth nearby where you can reach it with your eyes closed. Now breathe through your mouth and pour the egg-honey-rainwater mixture over your head and let it drip down your body. You'll probably want to scream while this is happening. Make it melodic honey.

Now some of you are freaking. You're saying, "Teish, really! Eggs and honey?!!" Listen girlfriend, it's actually quite nice. Water dilutes the texture of the egg yolk. The white of eggs is the slimy part and we're not using that here. The honey is smooth and the oil soaks into your skin, leaving a nice subtle smell. Many expensive cosmetics contain eggs and honey.

Besides, you get to read the ritual in advance and you know when you are going to pour the mixture over yourself. When baths such as this are done in my family, a number of sisters give the bath. The woman receiving it does not know what's coming next, and the pleasure of pouring the mixture over her head is always mine. So I always pour it when she expects it least.

Allow yourself to feel the rain of creativity and abundance on your skin. Rinse off with fresh water and dry yourself with the yellow cloth.

Remove the spinach leaves from your tub. Put the leaves and the eggshells on your compost pile.

Depending on how you feel, you can get to work now or go to sleep. The money you washed with should be used to buy paintbrushes, yarn, or other tools and supplies for your creative projects.

After tonight you can use the yellow cloth as a shawl, shirt, headdress, or lap cloth. Wear it whenever you are working on your creative projects. Don't be in a hurry to wash it though. It contains all the energy of the ritual and can be regarded as a placenta to live in while you give birth to your creative projects.

In my household the egg whites would be put to immediate use. But they will keep for a few days if stored in the refrigerator. I recommend using them as a facial mask. After cleaning your face, simply smear the egg white over your skin and lie down without talking or twitching for ten minutes. The whites will act as a mask, smoothing wrinkles and worry lines. Then rinse your face with cold water and enjoy the stimulating feeling this brings.

This ritual is designed to help your internalize the fertile energy of Spring. But rainwater can also be used to help lift depression.

If you are having an "April showers" kind of spring, you can alleviate some of that pain with a rainwater face wash.

The April Showers Face Wash: Sometimes we find ourselves caught between outer beauty and inner sorrow. Little green sprouts are budding, the birds are singing, people are walking hand in hand wearing bright clothes—and you're all alone. What a drag. Maybe you had a hard winter or you're suffering melancholy over whom you didn't get to see last summer. Whatever the cause, you find yourself crying at a time when the whole world seems to be smiling.

At these times it helps to collect some spring rainwater in a bowl, sit quietly, and let yourself cry into the bowl. Wash your face in the rain-tear water, then pour the water on your healthiest flowering houseplant. (See the figure First Rain of May on page 92.)

You see, the Mother of Beauty cries also. In my tradition we say that when Oshun cries, all things are about to be made right. The crying means that She can no longer tolerate things as they are and She is about to change them sweetly, sweetly. By mingling your tears with Hers and giving them to a growing thing, you make the statement that you too are ready to change and blossom.

WINTER

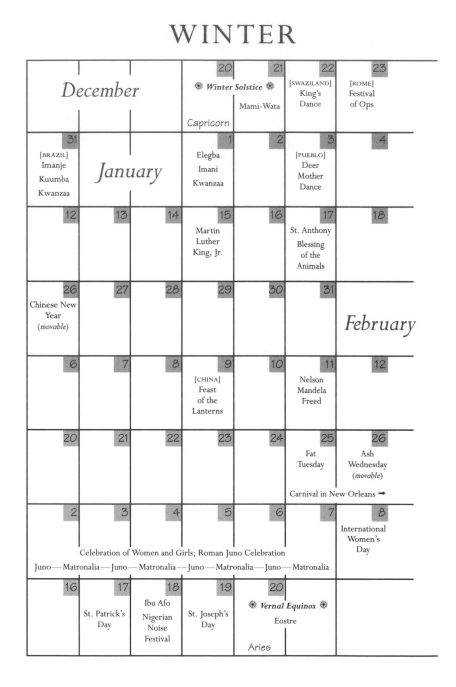

		20 ☀ Winter Solstice ☀ Mami-Wata Capricorn	21	22 [SWAZILAND] King's Dance	23 [ROME] Festival of Ops
December					
31 [BRAZIL] Imanje Kuumba Kwanzaa	*January*	1 Elegba Imani Kwanzaa	2	3 [PUEBLO] Deer Mother Dance	4
12	13	14	15 Martin Luther King, Jr.	16	17 St. Anthony Blessing of the Animals	18
26 Chinese New Year (*movable*)	27	28	29	30	31 *February*
6	7	8	9 [CHINA] Feast of the Lanterns	10	11 Nelson Mandela Freed	12
20	21	22	23	24	25 Fat Tuesday Carnival in New Orleans ➡	26 Ash Wednesday (*movable*)
2	3	4	5	6	7	8 International Women's Day
Celebration of Women and Girls; Roman Juno Celebration Juno—Matronalia—Juno—Matronalia—Juno—Matronalia—Juno—Matronalia						
16	17 St. Patrick's Day	18 Ibu Afo Nigerian Noise Festival	19 St. Joseph's Day	20 ☀ *Vernal Equinox* ☀ Eostre Aries	

Mother of the Night

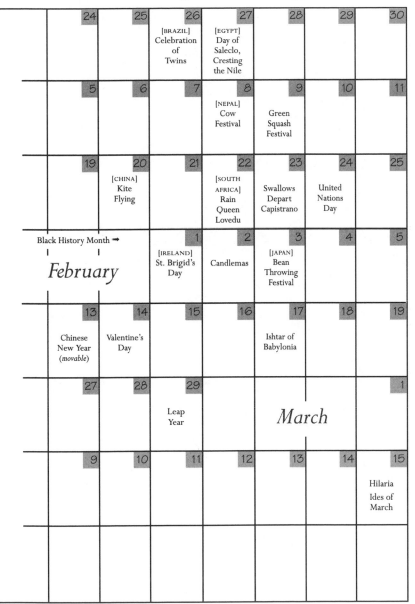

24	25	26	27	28	29	30
		[BRAZIL] Celebration of Twins	[EGYPT] Day of Saleclo, Cresting the Nile			

5	6	7	8	9	10	11
			[NEPAL] Cow Festival	Green Squash Festival		

19	20	21	22	23	24	25
	[CHINA] Kite Flying		[SOUTH AFRICA] Rain Queen Lovedu	Swallows Depart Capistrano	United Nations Day	

Black History Month ➡

February

1	2	3	4	5
[IRELAND] St. Brigid's Day	Candlemas	[JAPAN] Bean Throwing Festival		

13	14	15	16	17	18	19
Chinese New Year (*movable*)	Valentine's Day			Ishtar of Babylonia		

27	28	29				1
		Leap Year		**March**		

9	10	11	12	13	14	15
						Hilaria Ides of March

113

SPRING

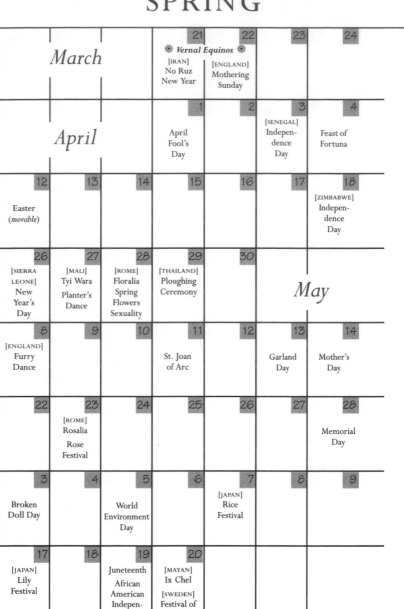

			21	22	23	24
March			☀ *Vernal Equinox* ☀ [IRAN] No Ruz New Year	[ENGLAND] Mothering Sunday		
			1	2	3	4
April			April Fool's Day		[SENEGAL] Independence Day	Feast of Fortuna
12	13	14	15	16	17	18
Easter (*movable*)						[ZIMBABWE] Independence Day
26	27	28	29	30		
[SIERRA LEONE] New Year's Day	[MALI] Tyi Wara Planter's Dance	[ROME] Floralia Spring Flowers Sexuality	[THAILAND] Ploughing Ceremony		*May*	
8	9	10	11	12	13	14
[ENGLAND] Furry Dance			St. Joan of Arc		Garland Day	Mother's Day
22	23	24	25	26	27	28
	[ROME] Rosalia Rose Festival					Memorial Day
3	4	5	6	7	8	9
Broken Doll Day		World Environment Day		[JAPAN] Rice Festival		
17	18	19	20			
[JAPAN] Lily Festival		Juneteenth African American Independence Day	[MAYAN] Ix Chel [SWEDEN] Festival of Midsommar			

Daughter of Promise

25	26	27	28	29	30	31
		[ASIA] Kwan yin	[BURKINA FASO] Bobo Masquerade			
5 Palm Sunday (*movable*)	**6** [CHINA] Qing Ming Ancestor Reverence Day	**7** Palm Sunday (*movable*)	**8** [HAITI] Ra-Ra Festival	**9** Good Friday (*movable*)	**10**	**11**
19 [BALI] Women's Fertility Day	**20**	**21**	**22** Earth Day	**23** St. George's Day Festival of the Green Man	**24**	**25**
1 Floralia May Day International Workers' Day	**2** [PHILIPPINES] Our Lady of Peace and Good Voyages	**3** [ROME] Bona Dea Feast of the Good Goddess	**4**	**5** [GUATEMALA] Rain Ceremony	**6**	**7**
15 [ROME] Day of Vesta	**16**	**17** St. Clara's Day	**18** [ALGERIA] Ibeji Ceremony	**19** Malcolm X	**20**	**21**
29 [ISLAMIC] Ramadan	**30** [PUEBLO, NEW MEXICO] Corn and Flag Dance	**31**	*June*	**1**	**2** [MALAYSIA] Gawai Payak Rice Festival	
10	**11**	**12**	**13**	**14**	**15**	**16** [EGYPT] Night of the Drop Hathor, Sirius

SUMMER

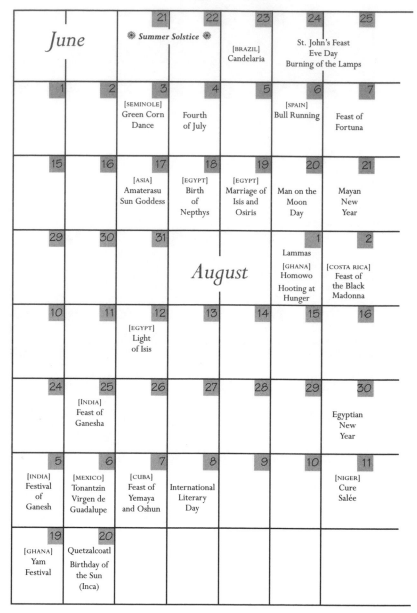

June			21 Summer Solstice	22	23 [BRAZIL] Candelaria	24 St. John's Feast Eve Day Burning of the Lamps	25
	1	2	3 [SEMINOLE] Green Corn Dance	4 Fourth of July	5	6 [SPAIN] Bull Running	7 Feast of Fortuna
	15	16	17 [ASIA] Amaterasu Sun Goddess	18 [EGYPT] Birth of Nepthys	19 [EGYPT] Marriage of Isis and Osiris	20 Man on the Moon Day	21 Mayan New Year
	29	30	31	August		1 Lammas [GHANA] Homowo Hooting at Hunger	2 [COSTA RICA] Feast of the Black Madonna
	10	11	12 [EGYPT] Light of Isis	13	14	15	16
	24	25 [INDIA] Feast of Ganesha	26	27	28	29	30 Egyptian New Year
	5 [INDIA] Festival of Ganesh	6 [MEXICO] Tonantzin Virgen de Guadalupe	7 [CUBA] Feast of Yemaya and Oshun	8 International Literary Day	9	10	11 [NIGER] Cure Salée
	19 [GHANA] Yam Festival	20 Quetzalcoatl Birthday of the Sun (Inca)					

Bride of Summer

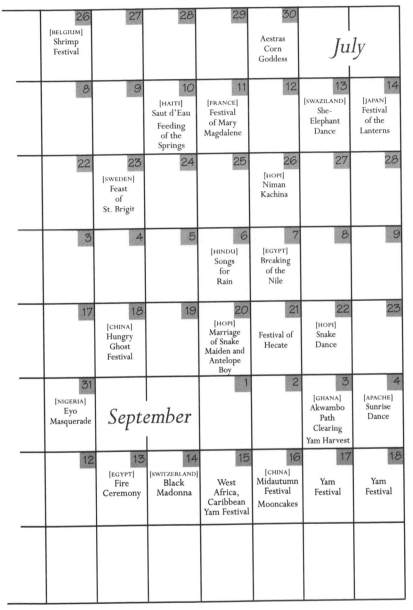

26 [BELGIUM] Shrimp Festival	**27**	**28**	**29**	**30** Aestras Corn Goddess	*July*	
8	**9**	**10** [HAITI] Saut d'Eau Feeding of the Springs	**11** [FRANCE] Festival of Mary Magdalene	**12**	**13** [SWAZILAND] She-Elephant Dance	**14** [JAPAN] Festival of the Lanterns
22	**23** [SWEDEN] Feast of St. Brigit	**24**	**25**	**26** [HOPI] Niman Kachina	**27**	**28**
3	**4**	**5**	**6** [HINDU] Songs for Rain	**7** [EGYPT] Breaking of the Nile	**8**	**9**
17	**18** [CHINA] Hungry Ghost Festival	**19**	**20** [HOPI] Marriage of Snake Maiden and Antelope Boy	**21** Festival of Hecate	**22** [HOPI] Snake Dance	**23**
31 [NIGERIA] Eyo Masquerade	*September*		**1**	**2**	**3** [GHANA] Akwambo Path Clearing Yam Harvest	**4** [APACHE] Sunrise Dance
12	**13** [EGYPT] Fire Ceremony	**14** [SWITZERLAND] Black Madonna	**15** West Africa, Caribbean Yam Festival	**16** [CHINA] Midautumn Festival Mooncakes	**17** Yam Festival	**18** Yam Festival

AUTUMN

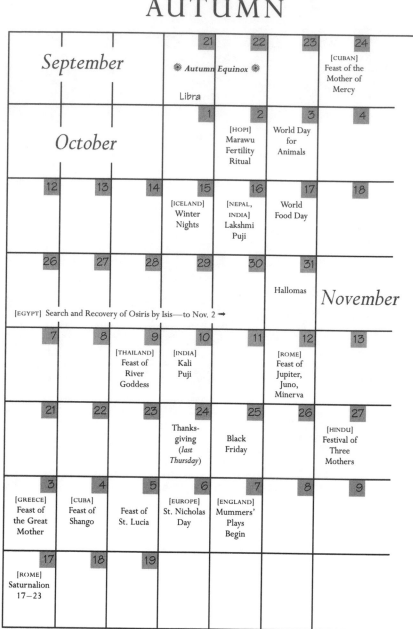

September			21 ☀ Autumn Equinox ☀ Libra	22	23	24 [CUBAN] Feast of the Mother of Mercy
October			1	2 [HOPI] Marawu Fertility Ritual	3 World Day for Animals	4
12	13	14	15 [ICELAND] Winter Nights	16 [NEPAL, INDIA] Lakshmi Puji	17 World Food Day	18
26	27	28	29	30	31 Hallomas	November
[EGYPT] Search and Recovery of Osiris by Isis—to Nov. 2 ➡						
7	8	9 [THAILAND] Feast of River Goddess	10 [INDIA] Kali Puji	11	12 [ROME] Feast of Jupiter, Juno, Minerva	13
21	22	23	24 Thanks- giving (last Thursday)	25 Black Friday	26	27 [HINDU] Festival of Three Mothers
3 [GREECE] Feast of the Great Mother	4 [CUBA] Feast of Shango	5 Feast of St. Lucia	6 [EUROPE] St. Nicholas Day	7 [ENGLAND] Mummers' Plays Begin	8	9
17 [ROME] Saturnalion 17–23	18	19				

Lady of the Sunset

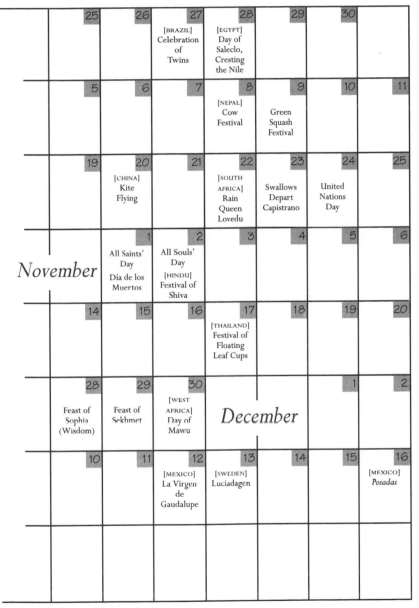

25	**26**	**27** [BRAZIL] Celebration of Twins	**28** [EGYPT] Day of Saleclo, Cresting the Nile	**29**	**30**	
5	**6**	**7**	**8** [NEPAL] Cow Festival	**9** Green Squash Festival	**10**	**11**
19	**20** [CHINA] Kite Flying	**21**	**22** [SOUTH AFRICA] Rain Queen Lovedu	**23** Swallows Depart Capistrano	**24** United Nations Day	**25**
November	**1** All Saints' Day Día de los Muertos	**2** All Souls' Day [HINDU] Festival of Shiva	**3**	**4**	**5**	**6**
14	**15**	**16**	**17** [THAILAND] Festival of Floating Leaf Cups	**18**	**19**	**20**
28 Feast of Sophia (Wisdom)	**29** Feast of Sekhmet	**30** [WEST AFRICA] Day of Mawu	*December*		**1**	**2**
10	**11**	**12** [MEXICO] La Virgen de Gaudalupe	**13** [SWEDEN] Luciadagen	**14**	**15**	**16** [MEXICO] *Posadas*

Summer

The Bride of Summer

Nanabouclou and the Piece of Fire

"In ancient times only the deities lived in the world. There were Shango, the god of lightning; Ogoun, the god of ironsmiths; Agwe, the god of the sea; Legba, the messenger god; and others. Their mother was Nanabouclou; she was the first of all gods.

"One day Legba come to the city and said: 'A strange thing has happened. A great piece of fire has fallen from the sky.' The gods went out with Legba, and he showed them where the piece of fire laid, scorching the land on all sides. Because Agwe was god of the sea, he brought the ocean in to surround the piece of fire and prevent it from burning up the world. Then they approached the fire and began to discuss how they could take it back to the city. Because Ogoun was the god of ironsmiths, he forged a chain around the great piece of fire and captured it. But there remained the problem of how to transport it. So Shango, the god of lightning, fastened it to a thunderbolt and hurled it to the city. Then they returned.

"Nanabouclou, the mother of the gods, admired what they had found. And she said, 'This is indeed a great thing.' But the gods began to quarrel over who should have it.

"Legba, the messenger god, said: 'It was I who discovered it. Therefore it belongs to me.'

"Agwe, the god of the sea, said: 'I brought the ocean to surround it and keep it from eating up the earth. Therefore, it should be mine.'

122

"And Shango, the god of lightning, said: 'Who brought the piece of fire home? It was I who transported it on a thunderbolt. Therefore, there is no doubt whatsoever, it is mine.'

"They argued this way back and forth. They became angry with one another.

"At last Nanabouclou halted the argument. She said: 'This thing that had been brought back is beautiful. But before it came, there was harmony, and now there are bad words. This person claims it, that person claims it. Therefore, shall we continue to live with it in our midst?'

"Nanabouclou took hold of the piece of fire and hurled it high into the sky.

"There it has remained ever since. It is known by the name of Baiacou. It is the evening star." [21]

This Haitian story is characteristic of stellar themes found in the folklore of the African diaspora. In the Haitian story the wise Mother-Goddess sends the great ball of fire back into the heavens. In many tales from West Africa we find a Sun-Father who retreats from intimate interaction with life on Earth. Often the Sun just gets tired and decides that He will roll around minding His own business. Sometimes He had been annoyed by human beings (they ate His clouds for dinner); sometimes they are annoyed by Him (His heat is overbearing).

The Western world tends to think of Sun-Fire as male and Moon-Water as female, but this is not always the case. Their genders are interchangeable. For example, in Egypt the Goddess Hathor is addressed as "the Fiery One, She who was never created." In Arabia She is called Attar or Al-llat, Torch of the Gods.

The Sun Goddess is named Anyanwu by the Ibo of Nigeria and "Indombe, the blazing heat" in Zaire. Akewa is Her name among the Toba people of Argentina. And the rising Sun, "the ruler of all the deities," is the Goddess Amaterasu of Japan. Oshun the Yoruba river maiden is the daughter of the Sun, and Mary the mother of Jesus is the "woman clothed with the sun" (Revelation 12:1). She is Sunna to the Celts, and to the Inuit (Eskimos) She is Sun Sister who took to the heavens after being molested by Her brother the Moon.

In the West, we have also been conditioned to think of the Sun as benevolent and the Moon as evil. But this opinion is shaped by our response to climate.

There is not much mythology of the sun and moon, for in tropical Africa the sun is always present and there is no need to call it back in the winter as men did in the cold countries of Northern Europe or Japan. Occasionally some of the gods are connected with sun and moon, like Mawu and Lisa of Dahomey. Mawu as the moon is more kindly and so beloved of men, while Lisa the sun is fierce and harsh. Mawu is older, woman and mother, gentle and refreshing. During the day men suffer under the sun's heat but in the brilliant cool moonlight they tell stories and dance. Coolness is a sign of wisdom and age, so Mawu is the wisdom of the world, and Lisa its strength. Sometimes Nyame, God of the Ashanti, is personified as the moon and represented by the queen mother, whereas another personification of the truly Great Nyame, Nyankopon, is in the sun and the King.[22]

It is safer to say that the Celestial Twins carry out the dual role of heating and cooling the Earth. The Sun gives soil, plant, animal, and human life the energy to expand and work, and the Moon gives us the opportunity and environment to contract, to rest.

Although the Sun is important to all life on Earth, in tropical climates *rain* rather than sunshine is the Great Gift; and the deities of the storm, Thunder and Lightning, may command more attention from the people.

Another Interesting Perspective

In the story above we are told that Nana was "mother" and the "first of all gods." Yet the other deities discover a great thing of which she seems to have no knowledge.

So we can speculate that at some time in the past, the Creatress set things into motion and allowed them to take their course without maintaining total control over their development. This evokes the image of the Pregnant Creatress who births a thing and provides nurturance for it without knowing what it will become.

As stated in the chapter on Creation, Nana receives a daily report of activities in Her creation. After its development She can exercise the matronly prerogative of Judgment. As the Crone, She has the right to pass judgment on the value of that which She has *allowed* to come into being. This is the dilemma of the Mother with the "imperfect child." In this story She returns it whence it came, an option not unlike abortion.

The Western Father-God is often thought of as a Craftsman, a Fleshsmith with control over His creation. Moreover, His adversary is the external Devil rather than the potential for good and bad inherent in each thing He created.

125

In the Creation Myth the Spring of Life, the Rainbow Serpent holds the Earth and Sky together like a covered calabash. This implies that they are interrelated and of equal importance in the functioning of the whole. The male Sun is *not* superior and the female Earth inferior, as patriarchal thinking has implied. This same Sun shines on the other planets in our system, but only Earth possesses *water* and fertile soil. Only She is in a position to produce and sustain life as we know it.

Contemporary ecologists are entertaining the theory that Earth and Sky are engaged in a cybernetic system of mutual attraction, interdependence, and interaction. This idea, named in honor

DAMBALLAH AIDA HWEDO

ILE ORUN

ILE AIYE

ILE OLOKUN

Ile Orun :
The House of Heaven
Ile Aiye : *The House of Life*
Ile Olokun : *The House of the Deep*

of an ancient European Earth Goddess, is called *the Gaia hypothesis.* A clear understanding of the Gaia hypothesis may change your view of our world.

Today there is much flurry about "saving the Earth." If the truth is told we are saving ourselves. The Earth has the power to swallow Her own surface, cook it in Her belly, and push forth new land masses that will self-fertilize and bear fruit. Madam Pele, Hawaii's Goddess of the Volcano, dramatically demonstrates this fact.

The plants remember who they are and reproduce themselves; the animals honor their destinies by following their instincts. Man is the creature who behaves with deformity in the Primal Scene. It is our own energy-consuming, Nature-polluting, warmongering selves that we must save.

We must alter our behavior (health) and learn to respect ourselves (peace) by standing in proper relation to Nature (conservation). This is balance and assurance of continued nurturance by "the Mothers." Be clear that we need Her but She can get along fine without us. Further, She has the Right and the Power to hurl us back into the Primordial Nothing from which we came.

Read, act, and pray that on the Crone's judgment day She will find us worthy of Continuance.

Egyptian Journey

I will always remember my years in the Egyptian Sun worshipers' temple, the Fahamme Temple of Amun-Ra. It was the beginning of a positive relationship with God the Father.

Before joining the temple, I'd attended Protestant churches and then converted to Catholicism. The Sanctified church was full of wonderful music and ringshout dancing. There were lots of ceremonies, talking in tongues, candlelight processions, and miraculous healings. But the elder of the church preached hellfire and brimstone every Sunday and painted a sadistic image of Jehovah-God. When I converted to Catholicism I experienced a different dramatic style. Now everything was neat, mysterious, and void of rhythm. I tried to comprehend cardinal sin, confession, and purgatory and found myself repulsed by the images of the eternally bleeding Jesus. I studied the lives of the saints, and Mary the Mother of God became my favorite.

My Mary was a tall, dark, full-lipped beauty in flowing robes who stood on the Moon. A crown of stars adorned Her head and the snake lay quietly at Her feet. She had a reputation for answering prayers and had spoken to children all over the world. She was a miraculous woman. A virgin and Mother!

My relationship to Mary was mutually beneficial. I prayed to Her and She answered me. But I still could not embrace Her Son-Lover. He'd given the world to White folks, made slaves of Black folks, and condemned Woman and all her children. I became aware of class differences. The pope adorned himself in priceless jewels while the poor struggled for food and clothing, eternally in purgatory.

So I fired the Christian church and began to explore alternatives. The Fahamme Temple was a wonderful alternative.

I was initiated into the worship of Amun-Ra in the summer of 1969. The Fahamme gospel holds Understanding and Cleanliness as virtues to which devotees must aspire. Study, fasting, and prayer were prerequisites for initiation. We were forbidden to eat scavenger animals, encouraged to learn martial arts, and required to pray daily.

Study was exciting, and lots of material was available. I could read, explore, and experiment. I studied numerology, symbology, and the principles of metaphysics. And I learned that these principles were universal.

My initiation was an eighteen-hour process. When I'd successfully completed this ordeal, I was given my current name, Luisah Teish, which means "Adventuresome Spirit."

I became the child of Osiris the Powerful and Isis the Mother of Mystery. I loved the intellectual stimulation but found little music and no dance directly connected to the service, and I longed for these.

In Egyptian mythology Isis the Queen of Heaven and Her brother-lover Osiris are credited with a prosperous dual rulership over the land. Under their balanced guidance the arts and sciences flourished. The people learned to chart the stars and predict the weather; to fashion tools; to cultivate crops, build cities, weave cloth, and spin magic. Lower Egypt (in the north) and Upper Egypt (in the south) were autonomous city-states. The culture was sensuous and strongly matriarchal, with women holding positions of power in every stratum of the society. Then everything got turned around!

"After the invasion of Egypt by Indo-Europeans circa 3000 B.C., Lower and Upper Egypt were united under a newly instituted kingship, and the Dynastic Era began. The invaders, calling themselves the 'Followers of Horus,' formed an aristocracy, or master race, that ruled over Egypt. The word *pharaoh* (*par-o* means simply, 'great house') was applied to the royal male alone."[23]

The Great Goddess Isis, the "Golden One," was demoted to Madonna the Mother of Horus; Osiris the Moon God became associated with the Sun; and the calendar was changed from lunar to solar.

129

Egypt fell under military dictatorship. The priesthood became an exclusive brotherhood, and "the male governors of Egyptian dynasties now pretended to have been created by a father God. He, Ptah, was supposed to have created the other gods through an act of masturbation."[24]

It seems that gynophobia and racism were born twins. My elders in the temple maintained that Egypt was the land of Black people in predynastic times. Now the world told me that the Egypt of my dreams was long gone.

Firewalk

"This is not it," I told myself, "and I am not the one." I sat in my seat of honor in the front of the room along with the other teachers. I listened carefully as Pa'risha, the clan mother of the White Buffalo and Rainbow Medicine Society, spoke. She admonished us that the firewalk was not for everyone, that one had to approach it without ego or fear. She went on to say that even the experienced firewalker would get blistered if she approached the ritual ungrounded. "If it is right, the spirit of the Eagle will guide you."

I sat there smiling at the students, listening to the mother, and running a tape in my head. I'd come to this campsite reverent. I'd poured libations to the ancestors of the land and asked their permission to be there. I'd fed Elegba, the Guardian of the Crossroads, at the front gate; I'd divined and received "great good fortune" from the oracle. My workshop on African spiritual traditions had been well attended. The ritual bathing at the lake had been beautified by candlelight, flowers, and song. I'd done everything I was supposed to do! So, I assumed the firewalk had nothing to do with me.

My inner dialogue was counterpoint to the mother's talk. Just as I decided that I would not even take my shoes off, she turned and posed a question to me. "Teish, how does a person walk through the fire?" The answer came out of my mouth without my thinking: "You just walk," I said, and I continued to smile.

We moved out to the campgrounds where the firewalk was to take place. I was asked to say a prayer into a large piece of wood and place it in the North, the gate of humility and manifestation. There were more than two hundred people, so when the prayer stack was finished the pile stood over seven feet tall. We added prayers on paper to the stack and set it on fire. It was a mound of sunshine, a volcano of blazing heat.

"Take off your shoes!" the command was given. My body obeyed but my mind argued with itself. Just trust the spirit, I told myself as I danced round the fire. If you really have faith you should be able to walk the fire. I danced in the circle, repeating the wolf chant and watching others approach the six-foot stretch of burning coals. If they could do it, I could do it. I stepped forward and the alarm went off in my head. "You stupid fool! How many times have you trusted the spirit and been *burned* emotionally, *burned* financially, *burned* socially and personally! Go out there and get your foot messed up, fool . . . fool . . . fool." The battle between the fearful self/one and the faithful self/one raged for at least half an hour. I watched the firekeepers add a layer of blazing red coals, and the faithful walked across easily. I reached inside myself to confront the contradiction and returned with a resolution. I would dance myself into trance and wait for the spirit of the Eagle to come and carry me across the hot coals. Satisfied with my decision, I raised my voice and chanted louder. Just then a young man who had witnessed my ritual at the crossroads the day before came up to me and said: "Iya (Mother), it would be my honor to accompany you through the fire!" I said, "Well, thank you very much but I'm not going to walk the fire until I get a message from the spirit. I am waiting for the Eagle to come to me." He lowered his head for a minute, then looked directly into my eyes and said, "The Eagle has come to get you, Mother. My name is Eagle Feather."

I remember hesitating at the threshold, being scared, praying, stepping forward. We walked across the fire, then stepped into cold water at the other end. I had no sensation of being burned. I got back in the circle and continued to chant. But the mind questioned, "Did I really do that? I didn't dream that? I just did that, right?"

Two people who had not been in the flame asked me to escort them across. Someone else inside my head said yes. Arm in arm, the three of us walked across the fire without being burned.

I rejoined the circle and thought to myself, "Don't press your luck." But this was a test and three times is a charm, so at the request of a friend I was compelled to enter the fire once more. This time we danced on the coals, holding a rhythm and circling like a pair of grouse.

When the circle was closed I went straight to my cabin, took a bath, and jumped in bed without looking at my feet. The next morning as I left the campground I went over to the fire, which was still smoldering, and took some pieces of charcoal. I boarded a plane and was home in a few hours. At home I sat down in a chair, took off my shoes and socks, and asked my husband to examine my feet. He found no burns, no blisters. I felt no pain. I was not burned.

I still don't know how I walked the fire, why I walked the fire, or if I'll ever walk it again. But the charcoal from that ritual has been ground into powder. Whenever I need courage, I paint my face with it and say to myself: "Remember, you walked the fire!"

The Quest for Fire
Political Power

In West African folklore the Sun is acknowledged as a great power but remains relatively aloof from the intimate affairs of human beings. The heavenly bodies, which are relied upon to shine daily, are recognized in prayer and may on occasion even receive offerings. But they are never regarded as totally controllable.

To really orchestrate life on Earth, human beings had to have control of fire. Fire, and the invention of the wheel, played a major role in the structuring of human social relations and the development of industry. Extended family and intertribal relations took form around the home fire; and the wheel developed into grain mills and chariots.

How humanity acquired fire is a favorite theme of world folklore.

> The Dogon tale of fire says that when the first ancestors of men were ready to come to earth they had no fire. The Nummo spirits, children of God and earth, were heavenly blacksmiths and an ancestor stole a piece of sun from their smithy. The female Nummo threw a flash of lightning at him, but the ancestor protected himself with a leather bellows that he had made to contain the piece of sun and lightning could not penetrate it. Then the male Nummo

133

cast a thunderbolt, and this also failed, though the ancestor slid down a rainbow to earth with such speed that he broke his arms and legs. Formerly these limbs had been sinuous, like those of the Nummo, but since that time men have had joints at knees and elbows.[25]

In a Dahomean tale Chameleon and Tortoise steal fire from Agba Kankan, a manservant of the Moon Goddess—Mawu.[26] And in the mythology of Native Americans it is the wily shape-shifter Raven who acquires it. In most tales, the animal or ancestor must display pretense, use cunning, or steal fire from the begrudging Sun; and like Prometheus of the Greeks, they often suffer greatly for having done so. Prometheus (which means "before thought") took fire from Almighty Zeus and was chained to a mountaintop where a vulture daily tears out his ever-regenerating liver.

Fire is associated with heroism; and in classical astrology heroism is the attribute of the sign Leo.

Although the Summer Solstice (June 21–24) actually occurs in the month of Cancer (the Crab), it is symbolized by Leo the Lion. The lion is the "king of the jungle." His color and mane are reminiscent of a blazing Sun. In mythology the culture hero often subdues the lion, and a brave man is referred to as "lionhearted." Leo is Sun-ruled, masculine, and courageous. But as stated before, the Sun is *not* always masculine, and the lion is not always the *Hero*. In the temples of Egypt, the lion was the property of the Goddess Hathor and was dedicated to Her son Osiris.

"The Egyptians also merged the lion with the Goddess, as in the familiar figure of the Sphinx with its lion's body and the woman's head. This figure is reversed in the fierce goddess Sekhmet, ruler of fire and solar power, who had the body of a beautiful woman and the head of a lion."[27]

Summer Seduction

June 21, the Summer Solstice, is the longest day of the year. Now the Sun has reached its zenith and blazes, in some places mercilessly, down on the Earth. She responds to His attentions with flowers in full bloom, and teeming wildlife. The human impulses of Spring are intensified and we flock to amusement parks, hurl ourselves into the Oceans, and make love in the fields under the warmth of a setting Sun.

In many cultures, rituals are performed to illustrate the Sun's effect on Earth life. Such celebrations may occur between the fifteenth and the twenty-fifth of June, thereby coinciding with the energy of the Sun's great increase before its inevitable decrease toward Autumn. The rituals vary from country to country. Some of them are designed to placate the Sun and to extract from Him a promise to return again. Some not only address the ecological effect, but also celebrate "the flame" as political power and divine inspiration.

June 17: The Japanese Lily Festival. On this day seven young women dressed in white robes make an offering of mountain lilies in a Shinto ceremony. The flowers remain on the altar overnight. The next day they are used by the women in a dance to dispel the negative spirits of the rainy season; and a large float of these lilies is paraded through town to purify the air.

June 19: The Celebration of African American Independence. On June 19, 1865, news of the Emancipation Proclamation reached the ears of slaves on the plantations of Texas and Louisiana. The document had been signed in 1863, but this information was withheld for two years. The end of slavery brought great rejoicing and fulfilled the prophecy of many plantation visionaries that "the freedom come" soon. Today, Juneteenth is celebrated throughout the United States; it not only commemorates the liberation of the slaves but also honors the contributions that African Americans have made to the world. These celebrations usually take place on picnic grounds and include historical theater, a parade, and a baseball game. They may occur on any date between June 13 and 19.

June 20: The Swedish Festival of Midsommar. On this day the Swedes decorate their buildings, cars, and public facilities with birch twigs. Each town adorns a Maypole with wreaths and garlands of flowers. People dress in costumes and dance around the pole all night long.

The time of the Summer Solstice may entertain a variety of celebrations in different lands, but the most popular of these occurs on June 24.

St. John's Day

He must increase, but I must decrease.

John the Baptist

June 24 is the Feast of St. John the Baptist in most Euro-American countries. Generally the Catholic church recognizes the death days of its saints as holy because their acts of martyrdom are revered and their entry into heaven is assumed to have occurred on that day.

But John stands out as the exception to this rule. His birthday is considered important because of the folklore surrounding his mother, Elizabeth, who was a cousin of Mary the Virgin.

According to this story, John was the issue of two righteous people, Zachary, a lawyer, and the virtuous Elizabeth. His father had been given the honor of lighting incense on the communal altar when he received a visit from the angel Gabriel. Gabriel told Zachary that Elizabeth would conceive and give birth to a son in spite of the fact that *her fertile days had passed*. Elizabeth, conceiving as a postmenopausal woman, can be seen as the Moon moving from dark to young crescent, the Crone renewing Herself as Maiden Mother. The old man was further informed that this boy would be "the morning star to usher in the Sun of Justice and the Light of the World."[28] When Zachary questioned the angel, he was struck dumb and remained so until the day the baby was born.

During her pregnancy Elizabeth was visited by her cousin Mary, who was carrying *her* miracle baby, Jesus. It is said that when Elizabeth heard Mary's greeting the baby jumped in her womb. And it is believed that at that moment the divine light of grace was exchanged between the two infants. This day, known as the Visitation of Our Lady, has been celebrated since the fourteenth century on or near July 2. At this time a statue of the Virgin is paraded through town as devotees appeal to Her for grace.

According to custom John was circumcised on the eighth day. Ordinarily he would have been named after his father, but the old man wrote on a tablet his wish to name the child John, and upon doing so, not only did he regain his speech but he instantly composed and recited the Benedictus, which "the church sings every day in her office and which she finds it not inappropriate to repeat over the grave of every one of her faithful children when his remains are committed to the Earth."[29]

A taboo against drinking liquor was imposed upon John from birth (as it was on the children of Obatala). With his sobriety assured, he grew up to become the author of his Gospels and the famed Baptist who washed his cousin, the Christ, in the river. So goes the story of John. But the customs of St. John's Day predate Christianity and actually have their roots in the Earth-centered practices of the ancient Middle East.

Isis: *Mother of the Sun*

"Sirius, Sothis, sacred star . . . the seven lights of heaven known as Au Set, She arrived to herald the time of longest light and brought with Her the gift of the abundant soil, as She raised the waters of the Nile, the waters that She had created from the tears of Her eye. Thus She commanded the blessed months of the Sothic inundation to begin."[30]

The Egyptian Calendar: The Egyptian calendar consisted of twelve months. Each month contained three ten-day weeks. A season was regarded as containing four such months; and there were three seasons to the year ($30 \times 4 = 120$ days $\times 3 = 360$ days). The additional five days that give us our year of 365 days were, according to Egyptian mythology, acquired by an act of magic, a game of chance.

The Days upon the Year: As the story goes the old Sun-God Ra was, for some unknown reason, upset with His grandchildren Geb the Earth God and Nut the Queen of the Night.

In His wrath the old man declared that these two could not bear children in any month of the year. But the couple sought and attained the help of the Magician Thoth, who engaged Khonsu the Man in the Moon in a game of checkers and won a 72nd part of the Moon's light. With this light He created five days that had not existed in the calendar before. During this time Nut gave birth to five deities: Nephthys, the Hidden One; Set, the Prince of Darkness; Isis, the Light of Heaven; Osiris, the Lord of Light; and Horus, the Prince of Light.[31]

The calendar was determined by the movement of the star Sirius, which the Egyptians identified with Isis. The Summer Solstice occurred in the eleventh calendar month, when Sirius rose in the constellation Orion, Leo the Lion. Osiris was believed to reside in that constellation and the Divine Couple were celebrated at that time. The stellar bodies of Isis and Osiris would appear on the horizon just before sunrise in mid-June. Then the waters of the Nile would begin to swell, flow over their banks, and fertilize the valley. And as the Lily of the Nile blossomed and beautified life on Earth, people lifted their faces to the Sun and celebrated the Summer Solstice.

The Bride of Summer
Erotic Fulfillment

In Euro-American culture June is the bride's month of choice. A June bride is thought of as more beautiful and fortunate than any other. This belief has its roots in the old Earth celebrations of Europe.

Pre-Christian Europe celebrated the promise of Spring with a wedding of the Goddess and Her Consort on May Day. What has survived of this ancient tradition is the Maypole Dance. A tree, sheared of all but its uppermost branches, represents the phallus of the Consort. Streamers of red and white ribbon are held by little girls and boys. Then they dance around the pole in alternating circles, creating a braid around it. May Day celebrants also make crowns of tree branches for the men and garlands of flowers for the women; these are kept until June and tossed into the Midsummer fire.

The erotic promise of the Spring Maiden is fulfilled in the Bride of Summer:

In northern Europe a nubile young woman is chosen to represent the Goddess and she chooses a bridegroom. These two are representative of the interaction between the Earth and the Sun, and the success or failure of the crops depends on their ritual performance.

In eastern Europe girls weave nine kinds of flowers into a garland that they wear on their head or legs overnight, hoping to dream of their future love. Sometimes candles are placed in the garland. The candles are lit and set afloat in a river. The lucky boy who retrieves this ring of fire is assured of love throughout the coming year.

In France and Spain lovers give each other a rose in a book; and the erotic fulfillment of Nature is celebrated with carnivals, parades, and dancing in the streets.

When this holiday was usurped by the Christian church, the romantic symbolism was separated from the Goddess and relegated to the June bride. The tradition of throwing the bridal bouquet was originally the tossing of the garland. And throwing rice at newlyweds reminds us of the couple's relationship to the harvest.

Placation of the Sun was an important feature of the Midsummer ritual. A bonfire was lit, and numerous offerings were tossed into it with prayers to the Sun. Wooden wheels or barrels were set ablaze and rolled downhill to imitate the decrease of the Sun's light. It was believed that by making offerings and enacting the

Sun's dance across the heavens, human beings could gain audience with the old man and extract from Him a promise to return after the darkness of the Winter Solstice.

But Midsummer was primarily a celebration of the Divine Couple, of Isis and Osiris, of the balance between Fire and Water. This symbolism the Church masculinized with Jesus and his cousin John the Baptist. The light of day decreases after St. John's Day and reaches its nadir at Winter Solstice (December 21). Thereafter the light begins to increase, and the Church placed the birth of Jesus at December 25, within the orb of the waxing Sun.

Turtle Soup

As people of different lands mingle, they adopt each other's celebrations. Each group attempts to acclimate itself to the energy of the land and to harmonize with the temperament of the other people. Each ethnic group brings its own unique flavor to the cultural soup. Ingredients from the far corners of the world are blended and give birth to something new that is very old.

The culture of New Orleans in the 1800s was European (French-Spanish-English), African (Dahomean-Congolese), and Native American (Choctaw). The Catholic church had long ago usurped the original eco-centric pagan holidays and turned them into saint's days. European colonists had invaded Turtle Island* and were busily exploiting the natural resources while systematically eliminating the original caretakers of the land, the Native American people.

The slave trader brought Nature-worshiping people from the forests of equatorial Africa and placed them on the tobacco, sugar

---

* Turtle Island is the Native American name of the North American continent.

141

cane, and cotton plantations of the South. In their Motherland these people had entertained a host of deities and ancestral spirits. They had developed a liturgical theater of magnificent music and dance, and were educated about life from an oral tradition rich in folkloric characters. On the plantation these people found themselves in a very different cultural climate but were able to bring their unique flavor to the soup even under severely oppressive conditions.

New Orleans Summer

The following poem was written in honor of the Calinda, which was traditionally danced on the Summer Solstice in New Orleans.

Bembe Ngoma

Once drum and dance met for a fateful date.
As heaven's hourglass of time had told.
The gods above sat patiently to wait
for drum and dance to sing songs of old.
As they began to baile[*] and to chant;
Shango[†]drums beat, Oshun,[**] she screamed "Miel!"[††]
Mountains rose to join in love's sweet dance,
and waters flowed from passion's deep blue well.
Danse Calinda,[***] the word was spoken.
Bodoum! Bodoum! bata[†††] drums beat.
An ancient African spell was broken,

[*] (Spanish) to dance.
[†] Yoruba god of lightning, power, and mankind.
[**] Yoruba goddess of rivers, beauty-love, and womankind.
[††] (Spanish) honey, sacrificial food of Oshun.
[***] A mating dance done by Louisiana slaves from Dahomey.
[†††] Bi-membraphones used in Voudou ceremonies.

as heaven and earth agreed to meet.

The angry storm became a gentle breeze;

and all the gods looked upon us: pleased.

(Original tale, L. Teish)

One of the main ingredients in the culture of New Orleans was the presence of Voudou as dramatized by the Queen Mother, Mam'zelle Marie LaVeau. She and her daughters did much to unify the women of New Orleans, black and white, rich and poor, pagan and Christian.

The Black Codes regulated the lives of Louisiana slaves and attempted to suppress the social and spiritual life of the free *gens de couleur.*

Congo Square was "the Apollo" of New Orleans, the place where the best Voudoun dancing in town could be witnessed. These dances were often raided by the police during a long political campaign against African religion that ravaged the city between 1820 and 1860. But the dances in Congo Square were performances staged for the benefit of the disrupters. The real ceremonies were conducted from Mam'zelle's cabin at Bayou St. John. And according to local folklore, it was there that she held her annual Midsummer Feast on June 24, the Eve of St. John.

The special drum be played then. It is a cowhide stretched over a half barrel. Beat with a jawbone. . . . The ones around her altar fix everything for the feast. Nobody sees Marie LaVeau for nine days before the feast. But when the great crowd of people at the feast call upon her, she would rise out of the waters of the lake with a great communion candle burning upon her head and another in each of her hands. She walked upon the waters to the shore. As a little boy I saw her myself. When the feast was over, she went back into the lake, and nobody saw her for nine days again.[32]

The dance performed at this time was a combination of movements retained from an African style of stick-fighting practiced in Trinidad. "An early version of the Calinda was danced only by men, stripped to the waist and brandishing sticks in a mock fight while at the same time balancing upon their heads bottles of water. As soon as a dancer spilled a drop of his water he was banished from the field."[33]

It is interesting to note in these descriptions that the men fight while balancing water on their heads and that Mam'zelle emerges from the water balancing burning candles on her head.

The songs that accompanied these dances had much in common with the Trinidadian calypso. Often the songs appear to speak of seasonal celebrations and sensuous lovemaking, but they also addressed political injustice and contained a call to acts of rebellion both great and small. Practically every city official found himself the subject of one of these songs; and slave women used the songs to declare themselves smarter and prettier than their mistresses.

This was the dance that celebrated the strength of the Sun and the sweetness of fresh water; these were the songs used to fight and to love.

The ceremonies at Bayou St. John could go on late into the night; but in the Square, when the nine o'clock cannon was fired in the Place d'Armes, the Sun went down for those who wore black skin and the slavers' brand. And the soup lost its flavor until they returned. Of this romance George Washington Cable wrote: "There is the pathos of slavery, the poetry of the weak oppressed by the strong, and of limbs that danced after toil, and of barbaric love-making. The rags and semi-nakedness, the bamboula drum, the dance, and almost the banjo, are gone; but the *bizarre* melodies and dark lovers apostrophes live on. . . ."[34]

Rituals similar to those practiced in old New Orleans live on in Puerto Rico, Trinidad, and Togo.

◟·

Summer begins with the Solstice on June 21 and ends with the Autumn Equinox on September 21. During this time the Sun travels through the astrological signs Cancer, Leo, and Virgo. Each sign is ruled by a planet; and the Moon passes through each sign in the zodiac within each month. The nature of the planet lends power and flavor to each sign.

The *Sun in Cancer* (June 21–July 22) is ruled by the Moon. Its symbol is the Crab. Both the Moon and the sign Cancer are regarded as feminine, watery, intuitive, and emotional. They represent the archetypal Mother.

The *Sun in Leo* (July 23–August 22) is ruled by the Sun. Its symbol is the Lion. Both the Sun and Leo bespeak a brightness, warmth, and generative power. Both are hot, dry, willful, and splendid.

The *Sun in Virgo* (August 23–September 21) is ruled by Mercury. Its symbol is the Virgin holding a sheaf of wheat. The planet Mercury is regarded as a catalyst, one who moves between the potential and the actual. The Virgin holding the wheat sheaf stands between the potential to create and the fruit of Her womb, the harvest. Virgo represents purity; Mercury represents process.

In Summer we experience the pas de deux between Moon-Mother Cancer and Sun-Father Leo that results in the fertility of the Earth (Virgo) and the subsequent harvest on the Autumn Equinox.

Whether it is the Sun or the Moon that moves through the sign, they share in the energy·of the parent planet; and their dance creates a conjunction of energy that has an effect on Earth life. That energy can be used wisely.

We can acclimate ourselves to the Natural Force through the manipulation of symbols and sacred objects, and we can direct the flow of that energy through thought, speech, and movement.

The ritual that follows is an example of one of the many ways we can relate to the Celestial gifts of a Summer night.

⌣· *The Summer Rituals* ·⌣

The New Moon in June 1991 found me on Salt Springs Island, British Columbia, telling tales of falling stars and talking trees to an audience of two hundred people, mostly children ranging from one to ninety-one years of age. I always request the presence of the inner child for storytelling events. Both the teller and the audience must be open and innocent. Performance and appreciation of the Art requires the Self who laughs, the one who is enchanted with life.

My weekend workshop, which began the next day, involved fifty women. Our ceremonial hut was a community center, a large cabin nestled in the side of a hill in the woods.

We played our "makeshift orchestra," smudged, sang and chanted, howled and cooed. As we went around the circle each woman sang her greeting to the group, introducing herself. We laid silken scarves in the center of the room and placed sacred objects on them. This served as our altar. Then we invoked the directions. Here I always call upon shy and inexperienced women to invoke the directions so they can see how easy it is and overcome their reluctance.

Working the Directions

East: The Power Osa. We began in the East, the domain of the beautiful dawn cloud, the place of the Rising Sun. Here we used *Osa,* the power of the Winds of Change, to help us blow away stagnation. We used the breath. The women were instructed to take a deep breath and to exhale fully until the lungs were cleared and the blood cleaned. With each inhalation we brought in a desired attribute and with each exhalation released its opposite.

We

Inhaled	*Exhaled*
Courage	Fear
Humility	Arrogance
Health	Sickness
Strength	Weakness
Confidence	Doubt
Wisdom	Foolishness
Beauty	Ugliness
Joy	Sorrow

This process continued until we could not think of any more to process and felt inspired to move forward with the work.

South: The Power Aina. We moved to the South, to Aina, the power of the Transforming Flame.

Each woman was asked to sit quietly for five minutes, thinking about her mistakes, regrets, sorrows, and fears. Then these were written down in the form of a request that these negative influences be removed from our lives. We acknowledged the part we'd played in the dilemma; we thought of how the obstacles had served us. We even thanked them for the lessons we had learned from enduring them, but became crystal clear that we were ready to let them go. This was a very necessary step. I insist upon this step mainly because people often love their negativity, wear it with pride, and miss it when it is dispelled. We had to mourn the loss of it before the next step could be taken.

A large stainless-steel bowl was placed in the South. Each woman was asked to touch her paper to the flame of the South candle, drop it into the bowl, and watch it burn. We opened all the windows and doors so that the smoke would leave the room. Each of the fifty women had one to two pages, so this ritual produced a sizable bowl of ash. We allowed the ashes to cool.

West: The Power Omitutu. We then moved to the West, to Omitutu, the power of the Cleansing Water.

Another bowl was brought forth, filled with water, and spiced with perfume. The women knelt on large beach towels, said personal prayers for purification into the water, and washed their auras from crown to sole. This act evoked the ancient relationship between woman and the Moon, the tides of the Ocean, the waters of the Womb. Each woman continued to sprinkle and wipe her aura until she felt light and clean, uplifted from the sorrows burned in the flame.

North: The Power Onile. Turning to the North now, we approached Onile, the Productive Power of Earth. A bowl of corn seeds was given a special blessing by a Native American sister, then passed around the room. Each woman spoke a prayer of potential, called for change, and made a commitment to growth.

The seeds were then dropped into the bowl containing the ashes, stirred together, and planted in a circle of soil in the heart of the campfire area. We sang songs to Ceres, Osayin, and Corn Mother, the deities of agriculture. The garden of hope was sprinkled with the remaining water from our cleansing bowl. A snake slithered up a nearby tree. Spontaneously women sang.

> Snake Woman shedding Her skin
> Snake Woman shedding Her skin
> Shedding, Shedding, Shedding Her skin
> Shedding, Shedding, Shedding Her skin.

The Wishing Stars

That weekend we were particularly fortunate to be working under the aegis of three beautiful stars: *Jupiter,* the expansive, beneficent Father; *Venus,* the Mother of Beauty, the Queen of Love; and Brother *Mars,* the Energizer, the Prince of Power. They were all conjunct in the constellation Leo. A Midsummer Night's Dream! This configuration, with a New Moon, held the promise of many blessings: good fortune, love, vigor, and style. These blessings could be ours *if* we made good use of the energies. The stars would be most visible in the northern sky at midnight. So we decided to wander off for dinner and a nap and to come together again at the eleventh hour. The night sky was cloudy, a cold wind blew, and rain began to fall. So we circled around the altar inside the ceremonial hut. We played more music and danced a bit to reawaken our bodies and engage our attention fully. We chose three candles to represent the three stars: white for Jupiter, yellow for Venus, and red for Brother Mars. We anointed and empowered them. We agreed to work the energy in three concentric circles of consideration: ourselves, our community, and the planet Earth.

I created a prayer/invocation for each candle, lit it, and passed it around the room. Each woman asked the light of the candle to grant favor according to the nature of the star it represented. For example:

White Candle: 'O Jupiter, Obatala, Sky Father, Benevolent King. We ask that you grant great favor to us, our community, and the planet in the form of [here women named their particular requests] 'good luck,' 'racial harmony,' 'the restoration of the rain forest.' "

Yellow Candle: "Lady Venus, Beautiful Shell, Oshun the Bubbling Mother. We ask for your love and beauty for ourselves, our community, and our planet in the form of [particular requests] 'a love relationship,' 'food for the hungry children,' 'the purification of the Rivers.' "

Red Candle: "Brother Mars, Courageous Warrior, Shango, Lord of the Flame. We ask that you give us power to be used judiciously on behalf of ourselves, our community, and our planet in the form of [particular requests] 'physical health and strength,' 'the tempering of male energy,' 'the longevity of the Planet.' "

When each woman had spoken her request, the candles were placed in a large pan of water. Throughout the weekend the candles were relit and the requests reaffirmed. Women were asked to visualize the manifestation of their request, and to dream on it, allowing themselves to feel the reality. At one point we each named and committed to the work we would do to help manifest the requests, and found that a lot of the necessary resources were available in each other! On the last night of the gathering, the candles were lit in the pan of water and allowed to burn through the night.

151

During this weekend we'd called the names of the Goddesses from all the cultures of the world. We'd paid homage to our ancestors by remembering their names and sharing stories of their deeds. We'd questioned the nature of reality, conducted the quest for fire, and reinvented the wheel. We'd laughed, cried, and danced. Now it was time to dismiss the directions, dismantle the altar, and go home. But I'd reserved a special treat for my sisters, a summer surprise.

From the beginning the ceremonial hut had been graced by no less than thirteen vases of flowers handpicked by local women. Lupines, Canterbury bells, poppies, and painted daisies were arranged in lush bouquets garnished with Scotch broom. The colors were wonderful, the scent enchanting. Four large bath towels were laid down and the flowers arranged in a circle around them. In the center I placed the pan of water that contained all our wishes made upon the stars. I instructed the women to step into the circle, three at a time. Each woman took a handful of flowers, dipped them into the water, and pelted the aura/body of another with the flower petals. This turned us all into giggling girls. The flower stems and petals were placed around our garden of hope. They would serve as mulch and decay into compost. They would nurture the hopes and wishes we'd planted.

The ritual above is tuned specifically to a beautiful alignment of powerful planets that occurred during that particular Summer.

Although Summer nights are the most romantic, the Ocean in the Sky brings us waves of power every night of the year.

The chart shown here provides basic information for creating stellar rituals according to the texture and tide of the night sky and your specific need. The chart can be used in this way:

152

A Stellar Standard

1. Determine where you will work. Whether it is inside or outside, smudge the area with incense and/or herbs that correspond with one of the planetary influences you plan to work with. (Generally, Mercury is a good choice.)

2. Form a circle, stretch and breathe. Feel your connection to the Earth and the Sky by stomping your feet and reaching for the heavens.

3. Invoke the center and the four directions, associating each with the energy of a particular element, planet, or sign.

Example

Center: Earth, the place on which you stand and from which you perceive the Universe. Or Sun, your own sense of Being. The Sun sign of the month in which you are performing the ritual, or your own birth sign. All these will serve to center your affairs.

East: Mercury. Air. Libra. These symbolize movement, thought, beginnings, freedom, and a call for balance.

South: Sun. Fire. Aries. These symbolize the will, power, and courage to move forward.

West: Moon. Water. Cancer. These symbolize the instinct to nurture, dream, and develop.

North: Saturn. Earth. Capricorn. These symbolize the discipline to bring the work to fruition.

Face each direction as you invoke the power and visualize places in Nature where that energy manifests: a windswept field, an erupting volcano, the seashore, a mountaintop. In this example I've chosen the cardinal signs Libra, Aries, Cancer, and Capricorn because they have the most power to balance, initiate, nurture, and define; and though I recommend their use, you may follow your own leanings in this regard.

Once you have created a calabash of energy in which to function, call for the assistance of kind spirits, benevolent ancestors, and appropriate deities. Deities associated with the planets are included in the chart; add to this list according to the cultures of the people involved in the ritual.

You may use a specific number of colored candles, anoint yourself and the candles with the recommended oil, burn the suggested incense, lay a configuration of gemstones on the altar, and create invocations asking for a particular blessing.

Example

Hey Ms. Venus, Queen of Stars
And Her Lover-Consort Mars
send old Hermes on his way
bring my lover back today!

You may hum, chant, dance, or sit quietly. The important thing is that you externalize your intention in clear symbols and open yourself to the energy of the Natural Force.

Always thank the planets for their existence and for requested blessings that you have already received.

This ritual format can be applied to any stellar correspondence—Egyptian, Mayan, Chinese, or West African. There is a mistaken notion among the uninformed that African people did not practice astrology. On the contrary, there are many astrological systems operating in the villages of the Motherland. Of especial interest is Gede, the Yoruba system within Ifa based on the power lines in the Earth and a five-day calendar. (Even a superficial examination of Gede is beyond the scope of this book, but serious students of Ifa are advised to consult the Odu Oturupon-Otura.)

Planet	Symbol	Candle Color	Oil Scent	Gemstone
Sun	☉	1 gold orange	dragon's blood frankincense	amber
Moon	☽	2 blue silver	lotus myrrh	moonstone
Mercury	☿	5 blue violet	patchouli mint	sapphire
Venus	♀	6 yellow green	cinnamon honeysuckle	rose quartz
Mars	♂	9 red	copal carnation	bloodstone
Jupiter	♃	3 white purple	sage cedar	amethyst
Saturn	♄	8 brown green	sandalwood magnolia	onyx
Uranus	♅	4 blue-gray	pine lavender	lapis lazuli
Neptune	♆	7 blue-pink	acacia jasmine	jade
Pluto	♇	9 black	rosemary gardenia	obsidian

Attribute	Holy Day	Astrological Sign and Associated Deities
will generative power	Sunday	Leo Olofi, Lisa, Apollo, Sun-Father
instinct intuition nurturance	Monday	Cancer Juno-Hera, Yemonja, Mawu, Nana Buluku, Grandmother
intellect change communication	Wednesday	Gemini, Virgo Hermes, Legba, Eshu, Janus
desire beauty creativity	Friday	Taurus, Libra Aphrodite, Erzulie, Oshun Spring Maiden
courage strength victory	Tuesday	Aries Shango, Heuyoso
faith expansion joy	Thursday	Sagittarius Zeus, Obatala
responsibility	Saturday	Capricorn Babalu-aiye
awakening	Sunday	Aquarius Oya, Hecate, Athena Damballah and Aida Hwedo
consciousness	Monday	Pisces Poseidon, Olokun, Agwe
transformation	Tuesday	Scorpio Hades, Ogun

Autumn

Lady of the Sunset

Oriki Oya

Iba Oya	Praise to the Spirit of the Wind.
Iba Yansa	Praise to the Mother of Nine.
Ayaba 'won obinrin	Queen of the women
mo be yin.	save me.
Ajalaiye fun alafia	Winds of the Earth bring health.
Ajalorun fun ire	Winds of the Heavens bring Fortune.
Oya Yansa wini wini	The Wind Mother is Wondrous.
Ase, Ase, Ase.	It is so, so be it, so it is.

L. Teish, November 1992

Softly a whistle rises in the wind, gently the dust broom sweeps. Leaves rustle against the Earth. She rises, growing stronger, standing taller, pushing farther, yielding more. Oya, Queen of the Winds of Change.

Long and swift She dances through our lives, hurling lightning, spitting fire, as furiously torrential rains fall. We reap the harvest; we grab the shafts of wheat and rip them from the soil. Oya, Mother of Transformation, we work so well for Her.

Lady of the Sunset. It is She who paints the leaves in Autumn; the hum of locusts is Her song. Her nine heads, the River Niger are adorned with a necklace of human heads. There in the cemetery She dances, dances among the tombstones with Her Sisters at Her side. There in Her garden leaves and seeds fly, rain falls upon the Earth. Death and Life rustle in the Wind, the seasons change and we who are Dead reborn must worship Her.

Goddess of the Winds of Change

Oya's power is most obvious when manifested through the tumultuous weather changes that occur in Autumn. By fanning Her skirt
of Autumn leaves and dried palm fronds, Oya produces tornadoes,
earthquakes, and hurricanes. She is the dutiful Mother of Catastro-
phe, the one who destroys outworn structures and sweeps away
debris.

As the tempestuous Queen of Lightning, Her husband is
Shango the Lord of Thunder. Together they herald the storms so
revered in tropical climates. Oya marries a fierce man but She is
fiercer than Her husband.

She is honored in Nigeria, the Caribbean, and Brazil. In Haiti
She is known as Maman Brigitte, the wife of Baron Samedi and
friend of Ghede-Nibo. There She has authority over the graves of
women. In India She is feared and revered as Kali-Ma the Mother
of Destruction. She can be associated with the awesome Medusa
and with Hecate of the Greeks. She is similar to Pele, Hawaii's
Goddess of the Volcano. She is Coaticue of the Aztecs, wearing a
skirt made of serpents and a necklace of hands and hearts. It is She
who raises the dust devil, causing whirlwinds and earthquakes with
Her dance. She is also known as Changing Woman among Native
North Americans. Fire, Wind, and Water—She is called by many
names. In the pantheon of the Egyptians She is Nephthys, the Revealer.

Oya is the dark of the Moon, the Boss Lady of the Cemetery.
When Her friend Iku (Death) visits, the last breath exhaled from
the body is captured in Her winds. Then She takes the soul of the
dead on Her wings and delivers it to the land of the ancestors.

161

In Her season as we harvest pumpkin, corn, and grain we are reminded of our mortality, of the continuing cycle of reap-rest-and-sow, reap-rest-and-sow. In this season many cultures celebrate the harvest and pay homage to their dead.

September Harvests

September 4: North America. Sunrise Dance. At this time of the year White Mountain Apache maidens adorn themselves in buckskin and feathers in honor of Changing Woman. Their fathers shower them with corn kernels and candy as a protection against famine.

September 5: India. The Festival of Ganesh. The Hindu Elephant God Ganesh represents wisdom, wealth, and humor. At this time He is decorated and given His favorite food offerings to assure a bountiful kitchen.

September 7: Cuba. Feast of Yemaya and Oshun. These are the sisters of Oya. On this day devotees celebrate the Goddess of the Ocean and the Queen of the River with elaborate altars, fine foods, and a procession.

September 11: Africa. Cure Salée. The Tuareg and Wodaabe people are nomads of the desert lands of northern Niger. After the first rains of the season they celebrate the salt contained in the new grass, which is essential for the camel's diet. They gather to sing, dance, share food, and hold camel races.

September 13: Egypt. Fire Ceremony. On this day candles and lanterns are lit before images of Nephthys, the Revealer.

September 14: Switzerland. A statue of the Black Madonna is adorned with flowers and paraded through town, then left at a roadside shrine where offerings of food and fire are made to Her.

Mid-September Rituals

The period between September 15 and 30 is held in high regard in many countries. It is a time to celebrate the harvesting of staple crops such as yams in West Africa, rice in China, the sacred corn of the Native American, and the ever-popular pumpkin.

This is the time of the Autumn Equinox, the perfect balance between day and night, dark and light. Here the equilibrium of the Celestial Couple is symbolized by the astrological sign Libra, the Scales balancing Justice and Mercy. Then darkness takes over as the Sun begins its great decline toward the Winter Solstice.

This ecological truth is celebrated in a number of ways:

September 16: China. This is the time of the Harvest Moon. The rice and wheat are harvested and made into large, round "Mooncakes." These are presented at the festival, along with offerings of melons and pomegranates. The women who make these cakes sing in celebration of the birthday of the Harvest Moon. The cakes represent harmony and unity within the family. Also at this time a young girl is chosen to enter "the heavenly gardens," where she has visions of the future prosperity of the community. The night is spent playing games of fortune and rejoicing under the light of the Moon.

September 17: West Africa and the Caribbean. The period between September 15 and 20 marks the celebration of the Yam Festival in West Africa and in the African cultures of the Caribbean. In Ghana, for example, it is celebrated on September 19. The African yam is a large, porous tuber with white flesh and coarse skin. It is often pounded into flour, boiled and mashed into mush for *fu fu* (dumplings), or subjected to herbal compounds and incantations to become medicine and food of the Gods.

The Yam Festival

The first yams of the harvest are always offered to the ancestors and the deities in ceremonies that include singing, dancing, storytelling, libations of rum, wine, or water, and the lighting of ritual fires. Although the specifics of the ritual may differ from one country or region to the next, certain beliefs are held in common by all peoples of the West African diaspora. These include a belief that the yam contains some of the spirit of the ancestors; that it is a gift from the Earth; that it can impart to its consumer virtues such as patience and humility; and that, if not properly respected and celebrated, the yam will cease to be, causing famine, poverty, and numerous other ills. After proper ritual, the yams are shared by the spirits and the human community.

Native American Corn

Native Americans regard corn with the same great reverence as Africans do the yam. It is a gift of Life from the Corn Mother and is celebrated in a number of rituals. Often it is smoked in a hole in the Earth, overnight. This ritual is accompanied by song and prayer. The husks are used not only for wrapping food and other personal items but also for creating ancestral dolls.

The Season of the Witch

Growing up in New Orleans, I went to segregated schools. The students, teachers, and administrators were all varying shades of Black. Yet my elementary school textbooks were all about young white children. That's right—I was taught to read with Dick and Jane.

Dick and Jane had many things that I did not have. They lived in a beautiful house. Their parents never fussed or fought. And they went to the ocean in the summer. But most important, Dick and Jane had an Autumn.

In their Autumn, red, orange, brown, and gold leaves fell from the trees; the children danced in the pumpkin patch and windswept Sunday hats tumbled across the page. In their Autumn Dick and Jane visited Plymouth Rock and played games like "Pilgrims and Indians."

My Autumn consisted of wind and rain; it lacked the brilliant colors of Dick and Jane's New England Autumn. But my Autumn was special to me because we had the mystery and madness of Halloween, and Thanksgiving was the beginning of the deep cooking season when my relatives began their kitchen festival.

On Halloween night the entire neighborhood would make jack-o'-lanterns and set them on the banquette, in the window, or beside the screen door. This gave the neighborhood a warm eerie feeling, as if invaded by sinister watchmen with heads but no bodies.

Children dressed in their trick-or-treat costumes as Frankenstein, the Wolfman, and various local demons who crawled out of the swamp covered in slime and Spanish moss.

There was no need for parents to accompany their children because each block was supervised by the parents who lived there. In our neighborhood the tricks were harmless and the treats were sweet. People did not poison children's apples, and kids did not stray from the group. Each child was met at the door with a "Please don't get me, Mr. Wolfman" followed by praline candy and home-made teacakes. The children held open their bags to receive the treats, said hearty thank-you's, and began trading goodies with each other as they headed for the next house.

In my neighborhood there was a burly brown-skinned man, we'll call him Mr. Buck. Mr. Buck was generally a nice guy who loved to fish and hunt but who occasionally drank too much and displayed a twisted humor and disposition. One Halloween night he invited a group of young trick-or-treaters to come inside his house. He asked us to wait in the living room while he went to the back, supposedly to refill the big bowl of candy from which he'd been serving his callers.

We had waited for what seemed like a long time when suddenly Mr. Buck appeared in a white sheet with a rifle and a rope. We went into a profound hysteria and ran, stepping and stumbling over each other with tears streaming from our eyes. We ran from the house screaming and the block guardians came running to investigate the matter. As we described what had come after us, Mr. Buck stood in his doorway laughing. The block mothers declared that he should be ashamed of himself, while the fathers warned him not to press his luck. Some of the kids described him as a ghost with a gun, but I knew he'd dressed in the cloak and hood of the Ku Klux Klan. Mr. Buck stands out as the most frightening trick of all time.

The door-to-door collections were usually over by 9:00 P.M., and then the feast of pumpkin pie and peach brandy would commence. While Dick and Jane played pilgrim, my mother reminded me that her mother was Choctaw and that it was "a shame before God" how the white folks had taken the Indians' land. She'd end with an admonition that "it don't pay to be nice to everybody."

With the passing of the years, Halloween became less and less important to me. In junior high I lost my interest in costumes and candy; the whole thing became silly, boring, and best left to children.

166

By the time I was a senior in high school I'd learned to regard the seasons of Scorpio through Capricorn (October 24–January 19) with dread. It seemed to me that all my relatives, friends, and favorite people got sick, had accidents, or died during this time—especially the men in my life (son, uncle, lover). This still holds true for me today. Further, if these tragedies happened at any other time of the year, I seemed to remember and mourn during Scorpio.

My sophomore year in college (1968) found me deeply involved in the struggle for Black Studies, fighting to learn *and* eat with no time for Halloween and other "White madness." One time I let my guard down and attended a masquerade ball on campus. A fellow named Pete G. put ketchup and mashed potatoes in his mouth and came as a pimple. His big joke was to squeeze his face and spit the mixture all over his victim. The Black students didn't find this funny and made it clear that "we don't play that." In Black culture there is a strong taboo against pie throwing, watermelon busting, and similar acts against the sanctity of food.

The Fahamme Temple shifted my attention away from Halloween completely. We simply disregarded it. We focused on the Equinox with praises to Ra and remembrance of Isis's search for Osiris. It was not until the 1980s, after several informative conversations with Starhawk, that I began to regard Halloween with understanding and reverence. She helped me to truly see it as the Season of the Witch.

Starhawk explained that Halloween is more than a costume ball. Halloween is the time when Europeans celebrate their ancestors' return from the land of the dead. I have attended Starhawk's annual mourning ceremony, where people rip their clothing and call the names of their dead relations.

I've also come to understand that for Western culture it is a time to recognize ugliness, deformity, and death, a time for the culture to exorcise its collective shadow. These explanations gave Hallomas new meaning for me, and I began to celebrate it again in an attempt to bond with my pagan sisters.

In African tradition we greet the ancestors as we greet the day, every day. Reverence for them is not *limited* to a specific time of the year. There are daily rituals and several seasonal festivals for the ancestors as well.

As my involvement in African spirituality progressed, I accepted the responsibility of sweeping the cemetery, picking up trash, and leaving fresh flowers on abandoned graves as a tribute to Oya and the ancestors.

Over the years my spiritual family has grown to include people with different ancestral requirements: Hallomas, Día de los Muertos, All Souls' Day. Each tradition adds its cultural flavor to the ceremonies. The rituals of these cultures are performed in conjunction with the more traditional African forms of ancestor reverence.

In order to appreciate African ancestor-reverence practices, we must understand the African view of Life and Death.

Between the Worlds

Mother Africa is a vast continent. Within her boundaries can be found a variety of Nature that is almost incomprehensible: scorching desert, open savanna, dense forest, and great mountain ranges. She is Mother to the ancient elephant, the impervious leopard, the graceful gazelle, the magnificent ape. Here we find the mighty vulture, the owl, and the parrot. The rivers contain crocodile, fish, and frogs. The water, forest, and sky are populated with critters that fly, buzz, sting, slide, and burrow. Innumerable varieties of plants display sizes and shapes that are among the most amazing to be found in Nature.

Like Africa's land, climate, and wildlife, her people are beautiful and diverse. Some of her children have blue-black skin and dark eyes; others are bronze, umber, or sienna with brown eyes; and in the northern regions they are tan, olive, and vanilla with gray, green, or even blue eyes. They are tall like the Watusi, short like the Pygmy, lean and angular in Nilotic regions, or full-bodied and round-faced in the Congo. They have created many cultures, wear many colors, and speak many languages. But they are all Her children.

They have created a great body of folklore and innumerable rituals to express their beliefs about Life and the Afterlife.

It is impossible to catalog all the beliefs of the African continent in this work. That would require a multivolume encyclopedia. Even if we concentrated on one group alone, the Yoruba of southwest Nigeria, the Bakongo of the Congo, or the Egyptians of the Nile Valley, we would still have a great task before us.

Further, for this work we must take into account the people, nations, and beliefs that crossed the Atlantic in the infamous slave trade. The many spiritual systems that came with them were affected by the environment of the new land, the beliefs of the indigenous peoples of those lands, the dictates of the imperialist culture (the Christian church), and the general condition of slavery.

So we will consider here the common chords of belief that have survived in the Motherland and on foreign soil to this day.

The World is a Marketplace but Heaven is my Home.

Yoruba proverb

In the African diaspora there is a general belief in a multidimensional universe. This universe can be seen as having at least three major sections: Ile Orun, Ile Aiye, and Ile Okun.

1. Ile Orun: Ile Orun is a Yoruba phrase that *can* be translated as "the House of the Heavens" or "the dimension of the Most High." Often this gets translated into the English word *Heaven.* But this is a misnomer.

The Heaven of Western Christianity has been described as a place where the streets are paved with gold, where genderless angels float around on gossamer wings and the inhabitants subsist on milk and honey. This has no relationship to Ile Orun.

While African people have many views about the place of Existence before and after life on Earth, it is generally accepted that Ile Orun is a glorified Earth where existence similar to Earth life continues. Therefore, there can be a dancer's heaven, a heavenly forest, a place where departed kindred are united. Where one resides in the land of the ancestors is determined by one's lifework, by the circumstances of death, and, most important, by the rituals performed in honor of the departed.

Since there is no doubt that Intelligence and Spirit survive the body, it is safe to say that Ile Orun is a condition of Consciousness. It is a place of familiar surroundings, sometimes assumed to be on planet Earth or at least in its atmosphere. It is a home where one rests in between journeys to the marketplace.

2. Ile Aiye: This Yoruba phrase *can* be translated as "the House of Life" or "the dimensions of the Great World." It refers to Life on

Earth. Ile Aiye includes the mountains, the creatures, human beings and their dynamic interaction with one another on the surface of the Earth.

Life on Earth is not regarded as a curse or as the result of negative Karma. Being born human is regarded as a natural manifestation of the design of Creation. Each person who walks upon the face of the Earth is thought to have an original contract with Creation. That is, we have agreed to accept a human body, to walk upon the earth, to express power through personalities that are chosen and character (Iwa) that is developed. We have agreed to use our minds and hands to create, and to be rewarded for those creations according to their worth. Thus the World is a Marketplace where we bring our gifts, distribute and exchange experience and information, pay our dues, and receive our reward. At day's end we leave the marketplace of the world and return to our heavenly home.

3. *Ile Okun* (or Ile Olokun): This Yoruba phrase *can* be translated as "the House Beneath the Waters" or "the dimension of the Mysterious Deep." It is a place where the souls of the departed reside before their transition into Ile Orun. For those who have not received proper recognition by their descendants; who have not had proper funeral rites; or who have otherwise been forgotten or neglected, Ile Okun can be a long night's journey into day. This dimension is believed to house the Intelligence and Spirit of the Unknown Ancestors, especially those who leaped into the Ocean during the turbulent Middle Passage. In Haiti this is called the realm of Damballah Hwedo, the serpent who helps to hold the Covered Calabash together.

Further, this realm is regarded as the place where the surviving intelligence of those unknown ancestors conjoins with the Forces

171

of Nature. Sometimes this produces an inherited family trait, causes recessive genes to come to influence, or fuels behavioral patterns that duplicate themselves from generation to generation. Thus from the House of Olokun one can inherit a predisposition for art, physical conditions such as congenital deformities, or mental seizures and alcoholism.

> The Universe is a sphere which may be compared to two halves of a calabash, the edges of which match exactly; the join line is the line of the horizon. The surface of the Earth, which is flat, lies on this horizontal plane. The first sphere is enclosed in another larger sphere, and between the two are the waters. . . . The waters outside of it are the source of the rains. But within the smaller sphere there are also waters—they form the sea. It surrounds the earth.[35]

It is generally believed that the spirit moves through these three dimensions in an extensive cycle of Continuous Creation.

Birth, Life, Death, and Reincarnation

So Life on Earth is an experience, a stage in the cycle of Continuous Creation. Death also is a natural part of that Existence. It is generally believed that one's natural dying day has been decided by the spirit, just as the birthday is decided. But, unfortunately, these salient dates can be tampered with, altered by circumstances.

The spirit of an ancestor who has chosen rebirth has as a first task the selection of an *Ori,* a head that will carry the person through this life. This earthly head *does and should* have constant contact with *Ip'ori,* the Eternal Indwelling Spirit or the Heavenly Head. The line of communication between Ip'ori and Ori is called *Ori Inu.* Ip'ori can be described as the Eternal I AM, who is cognizant of all incarnations, having full access to knowledge and power. Ip'ori knows the exact intent, power, and limitations of *this* incarnation, and sends the new person into the world with a body of knowledge, desires, abilities, and so on, that *should and must* be cultivated on Earth.

But during the journey through the Sacred Portal, the birth process, this knowledge can be affected. The child in the womb is subject to the influence of the stars, events occurring in Nature, and the experience of the mother and her community. For this reason African women are sometimes isolated during various stages of pregnancy. Sometimes the pregnant woman is placed in a special hut where rituals for protection and empowerment are administered.

It is generally thought that the incarnating spirit forgets much of its original contract during the birth process. The journey through the birth canal affects Ori Inu, and the requirements of the newborn (sucking, breathing, eliminating, processing light) occupy much of the Ori.

To thrive in the Marketplace of Life one must be reconnected with Ip'ori and the contract reviewed. This is the true function of divination. Moreover the channels of Power must be kept clean and open. The gathering, distribution, and use of *Ache* (Power) is the primary reason for most rituals. Because Ori can be affected by internal and external stimuli, it is possible that a person's natural death date can be altered by a loss of will to live, by accident, or by malicious intent directed toward the person from an outside source. When these atrocities occur and are not corrected by ritual means, we experience the phenomena called "ghosts." There are many rituals for protection against such interference.

African ideas about reincarnation are both simple and highly complex. There are as many interpretations of this process as there are cultures and families in the African diaspora. One thing we can say, however, is that these ideas have no connection with an unfortunate corruption of the concept that has become popular in some New Age circles. These days there are many people who bespeak a belief that "bad girls" come back to Earth as cockroaches and "good girls" return as raindrops. I have no experience of such beliefs operating in African spirituality. There are consequences for one's decisions and actions that manifest in this life and, if not ritually amended, may carry on into the next life. Further, the Karma of individuals is related to that of family, tribe, nation, the planet, and the cosmos.

African spirituality tends toward a view that is multidimensional. A person is thought to have a many-layered soul. It is generally believed that there is one aspect-layer that remains constant in Ile Orun, while a few remain close to Ile Aiye and others move through Ile Olokun and between dimensions.

There are simple and elaborate rituals being performed in Nigeria, Brazil, Haiti, and San Francisco in honor of the many layers of the soul. Let us examine the nine layers of the soul. Doing so helps us to understand our complexity as individuals and to appreciate our collective role in the Great Cosmic Drama of Life.

The Layers of the Soul

African people speak of the soul as being multilayered. The most comprehensive delineation of these layers that I have seen comes to us from the *Igbimolosha* (the Priest Council) of Oyotunji Village in Sheldon, South Carolina. The priests there have studied the beliefs of the entire diaspora and composed a view of the nine layers of the soul. I am indebted to those priests and especially to Iyal'Orisha Omi Aladora of North Miami Beach, Priestess of Yemonja, for her wise and humorous assistance in "cracking the ancestral code."

In numerology nine is regarded as the completion of a cycle; the ancient Maya believed that the underworld was divided into nine layers; and, most significantly, "Iyansa," the praise-name for the Goddess Oya, means "the Mother of Nine." Offerings are given to Her in cycles of nine; there are nine heads on Her necklace; and Her initiates require an additional nine days of purification.

The Universal Soul

The first layer is called the Universal Soul. It is that connection with Cosmic Force "which unites the human being with every animate and inanimate thing in the Universe." This layer is born out of the "Big Bang" that set the creation of the Universe in motion. Through the Universal Soul we gaze at the heavens and know that we too are made of stardust like the rocks, the trees, and the animals. We are humbled by the magnitude of Olodumare. We are awestruck by Eternity.

The Human Soul

The Human Soul connects us with the manifestation of the Cosmic energy in the *Homo sapiens* form. It reminds us that we *all,* who call ourselves human, chose this form with its gifts and limitations. This choice becomes a condition of Fate. We share "the total human experience" from conception to death. Recognition of this *should* assure our humanity in each other's presence.

The Sexual Soul

This Sexual Soul represents that part of consciousness that chooses gender. The intelligence that guides the spinning of the child in the womb (Obatala the ruler of all heads) decides, at a specific time in the development of the fetus, to become female or male. In so doing, one agrees to address the gifts and limitations of that body-choice and to share in the experience of others of the same gender. Thus we have age-grade groups, rites of passage, and secret societies based on gender. This connection is profound in women. It is a common experience that when a number of women live in close proximity they will often adjust their menstrual cycles to a common time.

The Racial Soul

This layer bestows upon people their physical characteristics and the "genius of their race." The Racial Soul decides what skin color and hair texture will adorn the baby. It also endows a person with the talents common to a particular race: a movement style, a contemplative nature, a predisposition for art, these things are often guided by the environment in which a group evolved. And although these talents may be inherent in all people, they may be applied differently according to racial temperament.

Fear and misunderstanding of the Racial Soul are the cause of racism in human beings.

The Astral Soul

The Astral Soul represents an individual's relationship to the Forces of Nature. This is expressed through the identification of a person's primary Orisha and/or astrological configurations. Here one chooses a personal temperament, which flavors the experience of Life in the Marketplace. The Astral Soul "provides individuals with special talents, proclivities, and adversities."

The National Soul

The National Soul is expressed through cultural and political identity and the quest for Social Organization. It is this layer that separates itself from the basic humanity and creates war; connects primarily with its own and sustains ethnocentrism; or extends itself beyond the boundaries of land and culture to embrace peaceful

177

coexistence. At this time in our development, the National Soul needs to expand to the Global Soul.

The Ancestral Soul

Here the human and racial characteristics are channeled through the gifts and limitations inherent in the genes of a particular family line. *This* talent or *that* attitude "runs in the family." This is the place where we find the "family curse." Sometimes the curse is physiological—an inheritable disease or neurological condition. But most often the family curse is psychosocial—generational incest, alcoholism, and so on. When these behaviors are repeated with fear and guilt, they usurp power from the other layers of existence and appear so large as to become a "curse from God." With clear commitment and diligent work, these generational curses can be healed.

The Historical Soul

The Historical Soul "provides individuals with the characteristics of their generation." It is a relative of the National Soul and can be connected to astral events. A particular generation (Pluto) can be affected by the political events of its time (Republican rule) and may respond to and participate in those events under the urgings of astrological influences (Scorpio: Sex, Death, Transformation). Children of the sixties viewed the world differently (free love) than children of the eighties (AIDS epidemic).

The Guardian Soul

The Oyotunji Priest Council describes the Guardian Soul as that "which controls, counsels, and protects individuals as they seek to integrate themselves with their other souls and the rest of the world. It is the Ori directing the fulfillment of Destiny."

These layers encompass Ile Orun, Ile Aiye, and Ile Olokun; they are a composite of our inheritance. We receive energy from them, participate in them, and contribute to them in the overall scheme of Continuous Creation.

The Family of Spirit

It is believed that one enters and reenters Ile Aiye through a specific family line. That is, one's lineage is traced through a biological system, whether it be patrilineal (father's line) or matrilineal (mother's line). African people created a culture based on the extended family, with a large and important network of grandparents, aunts and uncles, cross-cousins, nieces and nephews, sons and daughters. It is not only the mother and father who are important—as in the more property-oriented nuclear family of the West.

It is believed that this large group of people, the extended family, continue to serve as vessels of reincarnation for each other. So the girl child called Yetunde (or Babatunde for a boy) is bringing important aspects of the spirit of grandmother, mother, or auntie back into Ile Aiye with her birth. The possibility exists of bringing both "blessings and curses" on each return.

During the slave period our lineages were disturbed, and the names of many were forgotten. Under slave rule the forbidden was enforced. The slave woman was forced to mate with her own children and with strangers. We can speak of blood lineage for only a few generations. In our recovery from slavery we have reconstructed our kinship systems along spiritual as well as biological lines. Therefore, in the beliefs of this century it is possible that the newborn brings back to Ile Aiye the spirit and intelligence of blood relatives, family friends, national figures, and spiritual leaders.

Ile Olokun is heavily laden with the spirits of our ancestors. Early divination, sometimes before a child's birth, is necessary to ascertain the basic destiny and character of the child so that its development can be properly addressed. In some cultures the African woman gives her child full mental, emotional, physical, and ritual attention for the first two years of its life in order to safeguard its destiny and to assure the development of good character.

Good character is essential throughout life and after death. It is what makes one a respected community member and a revered ancestor.

Ghosts and Ancestors

If we stand tall it is because we stand on the shoulders of many ancestors.

Yoruba proverb

Ancestor Reverence: Each and every one of us is a child of the Forces of Nature. We are children in the sense that we are dependent on Them for our sustenance; but further, in the African belief, we are children because we are born from Them in spirit.

Sister A is a child of the Clouds, Sister B of the River, and Sister C of the Deep Blue Ocean. It is believed that each received a basic personality from a Force of Nature in Ile Orun and agreed to manifest aspects of that Natural Force during her stay in the Marketplace of Ile Aiye.

How well we fulfill our contract with Creation determines whether or not we will be revered as ancestors. In other words, those arriving from Ile Orun must exhibit life-preserving behavior while in Ile Aiye in order to be revered.

African people's ideas about what is acceptable human behavior do not always agree in every particular, but all have criteria to which descendants must adhere. The individual must exhibit the characteristics of the Natural Force that is his or her birthright. It is also the responsibility of the individual to develop character and commit acts that serve the needs of the community.

For example: Sister A is a child of the Clouds, born from the Natural Force known as Obatala. Sister C is a child of the Ocean, born from the Natural Force known as Yemonja. We expect Sister A to be creative, intellectual, and ethical. We expect Sister C to be creative, intuitive, and nurturing. We expect them both to be creative but in different ways. We expect them both to be responsible to their communities but bringing different gifts.

If they are both creative and responsible, each will be respected for the wares she brings to the Marketplace and each will receive rewards—both social and monetary—for her gifts.

If they have performed well in the Marketplace of Ile Aiye, they will be remembered and revered by the people after they have left this body. If they have done exceptionally well, their life stories become part of the folklore of the deity, the Natural Force from which they were born. Thus, in the distant future, Sister C's life story may become a verse in the folklore of Yemonja.

Now suppose Sister A uses her intellect in an unethical way. Instead of contemplating humility, wisdom, and honesty, she makes a *conscious choice* to be arrogant, cunning, and dishonest. She disrespects her elders, swindles her co-workers, and distorts the truth repeatedly. Soon she will find herself shunned by honest people. Her name will be omitted from the honor rolls of the ancestors, or she may be cited as a great example of what *not to be*. Oblivion and disrepute are what she has earned in the Marketplace.

It is important to note that everyone we encounter in this life comes to teach us something and to learn something from us. This exchange is constantly in effect. Consider carefully what you are teaching others by your action; be open to receiving the lessons that are your due; but, most important, remember that there are those who come to teach us what not to be. Early recognition of this will help you avoid a negative *Osa*-condition, one in which the Goddess Oya is believed to drive a person insane. In this condition a person can be thrown off her spiritual path through the negative influence of another. The person listens more to the words and opinions of this other than to her own head and the whisperings of the ancestors. When this occurs "your best friend is your worst enemy," as the proverb of Odu warns. The person learns to love that which seeks to destroy her, and a sadomasochistic relationship is entered into. The person learns to hate those who seek to love her, and a path of self-destruction and decay is chosen. In extreme cases this path is exalted and worshiped.

In the example above, Sister A made a *conscious choice* to be a negative influence. Now she is manifesting *Ori'bi* (bad head). The community will take measures to protect itself from her, and she will be regarded as a dangerous spirit in death. No one will offer to be her mother for reincarnation; thus she is threatened with extinction.

If spirits do not improve they will be forgotten.

"When have we ever forgotten to make sacrifices to you and to enumerate your honourable names? Why are you so miserly? If you do not improve, we will let all your honourable names fall into oblivion. What will your fate be then! You will have to go and feed on locusts. Improve: else we will forget you. For whose good is it that we make sacrifices and celebrate the praises. You bring us neither harvests nor abundant herds. You show no gratitude whatever for all the trouble we take. However, we do not wish to estrange ourselves completely from you and we will say to other men that we do not completely possess the spirits of our forbearers. You will suffer from it. We are angry with you."[36]

Clearly, little value is placed upon such a spirit.

Those who exhibit culturally approved behavior are celebrated as ancestors. Their life stories are remembered and their behavior emulated. They are placed on the shrines of the family and the village, and their intelligence is sought by the living. Ancestors may reside in Ile Olokun for a period of time. But soon the requisite rituals will be performed to assure their passage into Ile Orun, and some part of them will return to Ile Aiye through the womb of woman. This kind of spirit is revered in African ancestor rituals.

But it is the *ghost* who is celebrated in secular Euro-American Halloween.

The ghost is an unfortunate being indeed. It is a discarnate spirit. It may be trapped in Ile Olokun, but it is most often thought to float about the atmosphere in search of hosts. Its favorite hosts

183

are polluted or stagnant places in Nature, old houses where tragedies occurred, and the bodies of weak-willed individuals.

Ghosts are the spirits of those who died suddenly and unexpectedly (in accidents) or in an untimely and unjust manner (by murder or suicide). Further, the ghost may be someone who was neglected in life (a homeless person who died on the street) or one who has not received proper burial and reverence in death.

The ghost does not have the intelligence and creative power of the ancestor. It is much like a psychotic person, unable to think clearly or to take constructive action. The ghost is active and dangerous when it has inhabited the mind and body of another.

In the African diaspora many rituals exist for protecting oneself from ghosts.[37] There are rituals for controlling them, or for casting them out of your environment. Most important, there are rituals for healing and elevating some of them into Ile Orun.

Every Hallomas weekend my extended family performs a ritual for those who have been neglected. We sweep the cemetery, pick up trash, and leave flowers on the graves. In this way we minimize the ghostly activity in our neighborhood.

Guidelines for performing this ritual are given at the end of this chapter so that you may do the same.

Rituals are done to control and heal the ghost, but these rituals are not the main focus of African celebration. The central figures in African harvest celebrations are the deified ancestors.

Ancestors who are deified are generally those who personified and manifested the energy of their Natural Force in an exemplary fashion during their stay in Ile Aiye. They had a profound effect on the society in which they lived, and the stories of their deeds survive far beyond their generation.

The Deification Process

The formal process of ancestor deification can be traced to 3000 B.C. and the Pharaohs of Egypt. It began at about the time of the unification of Upper and Lower Egypt and impending patriarchy.[38] Of course, other cultures may have developed and employed a deification process earlier in human history, but no record of their beliefs survives. So we will begin with Egypt, then examine the cultures of West Africa and move across the waters into the diaspora.

Egypt

The Egyptians believed that upon death the individual (the Human Soul) would dissolve but fragments of the eternal within (the Universal Soul) would continue. The process of deification was that of accessing and preserving the deity (the Astral Soul) that existed within.

Those ancestors who had spoken with a "prophetic voice" and completed the process of manifesting their vision were revered and elevated to a higher status. It was believed that animals and plants also had souls and that all living things could be elevated to a higher status, a higher state of Being. That is, they could be reunited with what we have identified as the Universal Soul.

> From myth and legend there would seem to be ample evidence to support the theory that Isis and her family were actual people, perhaps from Atlantis or some other advanced civilization or even some distant star system. . . . Equally worthy of consideration is the idea that Isis and her family represented a parable of an actual Cosmic event, such as a shift in the Earth's axis, a change in the position of the Moon, and astronomical events.[39]

Each Pharaoh was considered to be a personification of the god Horus. Horus is often represented as a falcon-headed man. As one who embodied both Human and Animal nature as well as the National Soul, Horus was worthy (in the opinion of the people) of great pomp and celebrity.

The deification process included an elaborate burial in which the jewels, tools, weapons, and other personal articles as well as the wives and children of the patriarch were interred with him. The burial was accompanied by sacrifices of rams, bulls, and birds, and by proclamations and processions. The Egyptians also believed in nine levels of spiritual force.

West Africa

The people of the African diaspora were drawn from a large area of the Mother continent. People were taken from the west coast as far north as Senegal and as far south as Angola.

The inhabitants of each region—the Dogon of Mali, the Fon of Dahomey, the Bakongo—had their own ancestral societies and their own beliefs. The Dogon, like the Egyptians, believed that their ancestors came from the star Sirius, while the Ewe and Fon of Dahomey speak of their ancestors as the children of Skymen and Earthwomen (like Zeus, his consorts, and offspring). Other peoples may see themselves as originating in the Sacred Forest.

In Yorubaland (southwestern Nigeria) the societies that regulate the passages of Death, reverent celebration, and deification are called Egbe Egungun.

Egbe Egungun

The Egungun society attends to the business of proper burial, making sure that the death rite is fulfilled in a timely and respectful fashion. Funeral rituals reflect the status of the ancestor and may differ accordingly. The burials of an Oba (King), a Babalawo or Iyalawo (High Priest/ess), and an ordinary citizen will have some of the same basic elements but will also differ according to the requirements of the family and nation.

Masquerade Egungun

On special occasions the Egungun society sponsors elaborate masquerades to honor the memory of the ancestors. The performers are costumed in ornate ceremonial clothes, the entire body is covered, and the face is under a hood. Their mundane identities are a secret.

These performers reenact mythic dramas of the ancestors. The public performances continue throughout the day and the private ones throughout the night in a festival that is both joyous and solemn for a period of three to thirty-one days—nonstop!

Those who are empowered to wear the ancestral cloth have been initiated into the society and are skilled in mediumship. When the medium embodies and channels the spirit of the ancestor, it is a cyclical return to the original historical event.

The Egungun society also has the responsibility of implementing the deification process. The process varies according to the level of attainment of the body-free spirit.

Upon death, an inquiry is made, through divination, to determine whether the person satisfactorily fulfilled his or her contract for this incarnation. If not, those responsibilities may be inherited by a member of the person's extended family.

For example: A woman who was an initiated Priestess of Oshun may have had a contract to find a cure for fibroid tumors. If she spent decades in healing work, had several successful experiences with women's health improvement, but did not find the answer to the fi-broid-tumor dilemma, her daughter and/or apprentice may inherit all her healing tools, her case herstories, and her responsibilities. That priestess/ancestor agrees to work with her descendant *from the spirit world* to complete that work. This is important to understand as it is the basis for the practical application of ancestor reverence. Moreover, that ancestor may agree to bestow her healing gift on her daughter's daughter, who will then harvest the contribution of her lineage—thereby inheriting the gift of the Ancestral Soul.

The talents and responsibilities of a family line are planted, nurtured, harvested, and consumed just as are the crops of the Earth. Through reincarnation, human existence is subject to the same seasonal recurrence as the Earth, on the Earth. It is this logic and evidence in the workings of Nature that allows the African to associate the ancestors with the harvest. In this way the existence of the masses of good people is made sacred.

The kings and queens of West Africa were expected to embody the spirit of their lands, to carry the powers of their ancestors, to provide for the needs of their people, to be brave but humble, to accept counsel and make judgments, to live long and well; and sometimes, under the direction of counsel, to commit suicide. Royal persons who fulfilled all these requirements could be ritually deified through a prescribed process, their life and deeds becoming part of the mythic tradition of the people and their dramas reen-acted by the Egbe Egungun.

The same basic principle applies to great leaders, outstanding spiritual teachers, and extraordinarily creative artists. Usually, de-ification is done after death (immediately or years later), but on rare occasions a person may be deified during his or her lifetime.

The Litany of the Ancestors

The following biographical sketches will illuminate the lives and deeds of just a few of the people in the diaspora who have attained various levels of deification.

Shango of Oyo: According to various historians (Smith, Bascom, Ayedemi), Shango was the fourth Alafin (King) of Oyo. He was a great warrior whose organizational skill and military ability won him the throne over his milder brother. In addition, he was reputed to have great magical power, especially the ability to call thunder and to attract lightning. He could also breathe fire from his mouth!

Although there are at least three accounts of his death, all accounts agree on the outcome of his departure.

A well-known version says that Shango became jealous of two of his best soldiers, Timi and Gbonka, and forced them to fight each other. This resulted in Timi's death. This unbalanced use of power caused the people to become enraged and they demanded Shango's death. So Shango redeemed himself by committing suicide as custom requires. He hanged himself from a great tree and became *Oba So* (the hanged king).

Another version of the story says that while demonstrating his magical ability Shango overplayed his part and caused his own palace and household to be destroyed by lightning. Dispossessed and ashamed, the ruler took poison. A third version says that after a disastrous display of temper Shango rode his horse into the forest.

All the versions agree that his body could not be found and that a tumultuous storm of thunder, lightning (Oya is the Queen of Lightning), and fire followed his demise. Shango is believed to have spoken to Oya from the heavens, declaring that he had learned his

189

lesson and transformed himself. He had now joined the pantheon of Sky deities and would regulate the behavior of rulers on Earth. He became *Obakoso* (the king is not hanged), the Orisha of Justice.

Shango, the man, *embodied* the Natural Forces of Thunder, Lightning, and Fire, and upon his death he entered the pantheon as the deity of those forces. Everyone in Yorubaland is clear that the Force existed *before* the man, but the man personified the force to such an extent that he is regarded as being "at one" with the Force. The Feast of Shango is celebrated on December 4.

An Orisha as Natural Force before human manifestation is called an *Orisha Orile.* An ancestor who comes to be identified with the Natural Force is called an *Orisha Idile.*[40]

This deification of ancestors as embodiments of Natural Force is often misunderstood in the "New World," where lack of information about the African practice has led to some strange notions. There are people who insist that the Orishas are "merely" genies; that one must serve the ancestors and the Orishas separately or great calamity will befall them; and, worst of all, that the ancestors and the Orishas "hate each other." This is all so unfortunate and so untrue.

The principle operating here is the same as that surrounding Jesus the Christ. A child of God comes to Earth, fulfills a sacred mission, and returns to the Source. But the memory of that human being's deeds serves to guide the rest of humanity. (The genie deserves more credit in its own right, too.)

In Africa the Society of Orisha Priests and the Egbe Egungun may be two different bodies but they work together for the good of the whole society. I can only speculate that the notion of "hatred" between the Orishas and the ancestors reflects the guilt of slaveholders who raped and stole the culture and spirituality of their slaves. I have found no trace of this attitude in Africa; and older Lucumi (Afro-Cuban) priests have a doll for the ancestor on each Orisha shrine.

King Nzinga of Ndongo (1582–1663): King Nzinga was the ruler of Ndongo in what is now called Angola. *She* was the favored daughter of Ngola Kiluanji, the fierce and powerful hereditary ruler of that country. Ngola Kiluanji often took his daughter into battle with him. When she was as young as two years old, he fought with her sitting on his shoulder. Nzinga was trained by her father in personal defense, military strategy, and peace negotiations. She was a visionary who was also trained in mediumship, dream interpretation, and natural medicine. When the king died his throne was inherited by a son called Mbandi, a brutal and insecure person who killed his brother and his sister Nzinga's only son. A poor ruler, Mbandi lost much of his father's territory—and along with it the support of his people.

Between 1580 and 1640 the Spanish and the Portuguese shared the slave market in Angola. The Portuguese set up a puppet government in Angola and with the blessing of the Catholic church exported slaves to Brazil and Lisbon and colonized the people of Angola.

In 1622 Nzinga traveled with her entourage to the city of Luanda to meet with the Portuguese governor, João Correa de Souza. De Souza sought to insult Nzinga by sitting in a chair while offering Nzinga a pillow on the ground. One of her servants placed himself in position and provided his back for the queen to sit on. During that session she negotiated the exchange of prisoners of war, declared Ndongo a free territory, and designed a treaty.

Eventually Nzinga accepted baptism and a Portuguese education. She took the name Dona Ana de Souza and convinced her two sisters to take foreign names also. These things she did as a gesture of goodwill. But after observing the Portuguese, their long history of exploitation, their disrespect for tribal rulers, and their insatiable brutality toward the slaves, Nzinga realized that the colonizers' doctrine of "Christian charity" did not apply to the African people. She declared herself Nzinga again and in 1624 killed her impotent brother and declared war on the Portuguese.

She withstood the necessary ordeals of initiation. Thirty of the tribe's men brought her the implements of kingship, which she accepted. The sacrifices were made. She declared herself the rightful heir to the throne that would have been her son's. From that day on, she wore men's clothing, took sixty young and handsome men as her wives, and waged successful battles against the Portuguese. She was a brilliant strategist, using the environment, the talents of neighboring tribes, and the element of surprise to overcome the enemy. Between 1630 and 1635 she rebuilt the country and united the tribes as never before or since.

In 1641 the Dutch took over Portugal's territories in Angola and King Nzinga formed military alliances with them. She and her allies continued to fight until 1656, when peace was agreed upon.

At age seventy-five she released her sixty wives and married one young man, again as a strategic gesture of concession to European cultural ideas.

On December 12, 1663, King Nzinga died. Her body was adorned in the finest cloth and jewels as tribal custom requires, and the last rites were administered by a Father Cavazzi.

Her sister took over the country, and after her there were

many female leaders and rulers. The title Ngola, which had been forbidden to women, was now relegated only to women for many generations.

Today King Nzinga Kiluanji is celebrated by Angolan descendants in Bahia, Brazil. A woman is chosen to represent her in a ritual reenactment of her life. The people parade in the streets exhibiting skill in *capoeira,* a martial arts form inherited from Angola. It can be said that by honoring her in this way, the people have elevated her to the status of a goddess and are preserving and serving the Diasporic Soul. Nzinga is associated with Yansa, the Goddess of the Autumn Wind.

◝•

This deification process is practiced in many places. Chaka, the Zulu warrior who united South Africa, was deified in his own lifetime. In Haiti the Voudoun *loa* known as Dan Petro was an eighteenth-century *houngan* (priest). The Catholic church deifies (canonizes) its saints, as do the Buddhists.

In secular society we, by our behavior, make demigods of political figures and movie stars, and even romanticize famous criminals.

Both natural forces and ideas become personified through human thought and action. If the thought and action associated with an individual have a transformative effect on the collective, that person becomes a legendary figure. So today many people regard Mahatma Gandhi, John F. Kennedy, Harriet Tubman, Martin Luther King, Sojourner Truth, John Coltrane, Joan of Arc, and El-Hadj Malik El-Shabazz Malcolm X, (just to name a few) as symbols of Freedom. This is the road to deification.

And the swastika, an ancient sacred symbol, now signifies the degenerative cruelty of Hitler. He walked the path of demonization.

On a daily basis "little people" like you and I struggle to fulfill our contracts with Creation. On a daily basis we perform heroic deeds to preserve ourselves and our planet. With our gifts and our limitations we must strive to manifest life-preserving behavior according to the requirements of our time and circumstances.

As we stand at the end of the twentieth century we must realize that we are the "ancestors of the future." We must invoke for the Spontaneous Transformation of individuals, families, nations, and the human race. And we must put our best foot forward as we step into the twentieth-first century.

I believe that with the proper attitude adjustment we can halt the hand of extinction, send wanton war to bed, and live in peaceful coexistence and prosperity on this beautiful planet of ours.

If we perform our job well enough, our collective effort will be mythologized in the folklore of the future. Sow well, that we may reap a bountiful harvest.

Hallomas

During the Hallomas season my extended family honors the ancestors with a Masquerade Egungun. At the masquerade we dress up as a family member or a historical figure and portray the lives and deeds of those people in short presentations.

We construct an altar to the Goddess Oya and surround Her with an entourage of ancestors. We make a visit to the cemetery carrying "consecrated brooms." There we pick up debris, sweep, lay flowers, and say prayers for the spirits of those who have been neglected by their descendants. We hold special ceremonies for our own ancestors, with each ceremony reflecting the descendants' cultural background—African, Native American, Latin, or pre-Christian European.

These feasts include decorative altars and elaborate meals with breads corresponding to the culture being honored—*pan muerto,* cornbread, *akara,* or *njeri.* These celebrations generally begin around October 18 and end on November 2. The Women's Society closes the festivities with a celebration of Oya (Osa Ogunda) as the Deer Woman of Owo, a bush creature, who is the Mother of wealth.

Of course, during this time the rest of the neighborhood is celebrating with the standard American "trick or treat." All the houses have jack-o'-lanterns or paper skeletons adorning their front doors. A few people do not participate at all. They simply leave their homes and do not return until the whole affair is over.

At my own home I decorate the front porch with an Ancestral Harvest altar. I drape a piece of cloth over the windows, set out a few tables and boxes of different heights, and cover them with cloth. I draw faces on the backs of four paper plates and tack them to the cloth in the North, South, East, and West positions. Then I dress the altar with numerous pumpkins of various sizes, squashes, gourds, ears of corn, yams, and the dried roots of plants pulled from my garden. Next I place several of the sugar skulls made especially for Día de los Muertos. Four small metal bowls are filled with soil, and orange, brown, green, and yellow candles (in their glasses) are secured in the soil. These serve as lamps for the altar. The whole thing is sprinkled with wild rice and red wine. As a finishing touch I stick nine pinwheels in the ground around the yard.

Then I put together an assortment of nuts and wrapped candies in a bowl to pass out to trick-or-treaters.

"Trick or treat!" The little monsters come dressed to kill. They come as Dracula, Frankenstein, and the Wolfman. They come as fairies, as Batman, as Teenage Mutant Ninja Turtles. One very astute young man came to my door wearing a mask of Richard Nixon. Aha, a real monster approaches.

Monsters are born out of human fears; they are created in the image of the Racial and National Souls. While all human beings have fears, how they are symbolized differs from one group of people to another. The dragon that is feared in the West is revered in the East. Due to modern media, the European Halloween monsters are known all over the world.

The folklore of a people reflects their racial genius, their response to their environment, and their history. Not much is known about the monsters of the African diaspora. While television has done a great job of distortion, the real folklore goes unaddressed. For example, the mummy who stalks the land killing people is not an Egyptian belief. It is the fearful response of those who pillaged the tombs. And Wes Craven's ridiculous movie *The Serpent and the Rainbow* is a far cry from the book by Dr. Wade Davis. In his monumental work on the creation of the zombie, Dr. Davis shows that *the great fear among the Haitian people is not of being attacked by a zombie; the fear is of the real possibility of becoming a zombie.*

Since I cannot trust Hollywood to retain any of the folklore of the diaspora, I would like to make a small Halloween offering here. So hold on to your seats, folks: listen carefully for the sound of the drum beating at your back door. Prepare to laugh and cry as we enter the African Bush of Ghosts.

The Bush of Ghosts

The African bush is regarded not only as a physical place in Nature (the forest) but also as a mystical place. The real forest is populated with plants, animals, and mythic beings; the mystical forest houses the beliefs, fears, and dreams of the human psyche.

Some of these characters are genuinely bad news; others behave with mischief or medicine according to the situation; and some were originally regarded as good and powerful but acquired bad reputations because of the infiltration of foreign ideas. While an exhaustive cataloging of the Bush of Ghosts is impossible in this work, please allow me to share with you a few of my favorites.

> In the beginning God gave the World to the Witches.
>
> Yoruba proverb

The Aje of West Africa: At the top of my list of favorites are the Aje. *Aje* has come to be defined as "witch" with negative connotations attached. But like her European sister, the African witch is the victim of "bad mouth." She is the repository of female sexual power (that of life and death), spiritual and psychic power (shapeshifting and the ability to fly), and the economic independence of the Market Women (Oya is the Queen of the Market). This combination of powers makes her a threat to the idea of patriarchal domination.

The Aje are said to have a special relationship to the trickster-magician Eshu (the penis). They have the power to turn themselves into birds or other bush creatures. According to the folklore of Nigeria, the Aje are capable of causing impotence in men, miscarriage in women, and mass hysteria in the community.

But the Aje did *not* come into the world as personifications of evil. On the contrary, the Holy Odus (Osa Meji and Irete Owonrin) tell us that the World could not have sustained human life without the Iyamis (Our Mothers). But because men were found mistreating women, the Iyamis are perpetually enraged and must be placated in elaborate costumed processions called *Gelede.*

In the Gelede festival the men of the cult dress as women, sing and dance, and reenact the stories of the Mothers in order to placate their anger. This assures good weather, abundant crops, and continued procreation—the concerns of Autumn.

Aje are usually envisioned as older women, but young women might also be Aje. They are not regarded or described as hideous. It is generally thought that they attack when provoked and are not easily placated.

Gelede is celebrated in Nigeria, Benin, Togo, and other West African countries. Vestiges of it remain in Brazil and in the court of the Seven Sisters of New Orleans. But the societies are highly secret and I was told (in New Orleans) that "there is a penalty for asking about them." A few scholars have written about them (Drewal, Verger, and Hoch-smith) but the subject remains obscured in the shadows of ignorance and fear.

The Abiku: The Abiku is a source of great sorrow in West Africa. It is a cruelly indecisive spirit. It enters the womb of a woman, gestates and is born, then mysteriously dies in infancy (crib death). The Abiku returns to the same woman repeatedly and dies repeatedly, thereby torturing the mother and causing the family great anguish. Abikus are believed to hide out in the forest and may attach themselves to a woman as she walks by. The corpse of a suspected Abiku will be marked before burial. If there is a subsequent pregnancy, the newborn is examined for signs of the mark. If the mark of the deceased is found on the living child, the newborn then receives charms and amulets with prayers invoking the spirit to remain in the body to fulfill its lifework.

Sasabonsam: In Ghana, West Africa, the Sasabonsam is regarded as a bush creature of dubious behavior. It is apelike, humanoid but covered with hair. It has blood-red eyes bulging from its hairy face, sharp teeth, and long legs. Its feet point in both directions. It is thought of as both animal and wandering spirit. It collects lost souls and pounces on unwary hunters.

Duppies: In Jamaica duppies are very popular characters. They are basically disincarnates who are believed to linger around their own graves, especially if they died tragically. Duppies are given to hanging around livestock and are believed to attack cattle.

Hants: In New Orleans the spirits of people who died during pregnancy or by suicide, hanging, drowning, or sudden accident are treated with wariness. It is believed that these spirits are in shock, do not know what has happened to them, and are lurking nearby. They are reputed to hide out in the swamp reeking of slime and Spanish moss. They crave human bodies again and will pounce on any unwary passerby.

The Wild Ones: Throughout the African diaspora there are stories of bush creatures. Some are benevolent village guardians; others, fierce and dangerous like the Leopard Men of the Congo. The latter are a secret society of hunters who dress in leopard skins and carry weapons made of leopard claws. They are accused of attacking both animals and people who get lost in the bush.

Cochon Gris: In Haiti there is rumor of the *Cochon Gris,* the cult of the gray pig. They wear blood-red clothing and carry bows and arrows. They are thought to be the spirit disciples of Jesus who, under instruction, put him to death.

Of course this list could go on. But a longer list would merely illustrate variations on the same themes: Bush creatures are our animal nature, our connection to the natural world. The disincarnates represent our apprehension about the coming Unknown, the pull between the desire for continued existence and the need to rest. These things we all tend to fear.

But I must admit that these days it is the humans with privilege, power, and a bad attitude who bother me the most among the monsters.

At Halloween we cleanse our collective shadow. We allow our fears to surface. We dress them up in funny costumes and allow them to walk at night. We laugh and tremble, and celebrate death. Oya, the Boss Lady of the Cemetery, wields Her broom. The wind blows, the rain falls, old structures collapse.

In Autumn, the Sun moves toward the Great Decline. The Earth yields Her harvest. We gather up Her offerings. We store, can, and freeze them as a shield against Winter. We rip the roots out of the Earth, let the garden lie fallow. The time of fullness passes. Oya, the Goddess of the Winds of Change, parades Her entourage of dead. In Autumn all is reaped. In Winter all is rest. And all is reborn in the promise of Spring.

The Harvest Home

Autumn can be a beautiful time. During November we hear the whistle of strong winds, see vibrant multicolored leaves dancing in the breeze, and smell the aroma of cinnamon, nutmeg, and ginger. The Goddess Oya delights in these.

In the United States, Thanksgiving occurs on the last Thursday in November and is celebrated as a secular national holiday. But Thanksgiving is really the celebration of the Harvest Home; it is a religious event dressed in patriotic clothing.

The celebration of the Harvest Home has been observed by people all over the world since the advent of agriculture. Quite simply, people everywhere marked the time when the crops were harvested. This meant that the work in the garden was finished for that year. The food would be preserved and stored as security against the scarcity of Winter. Then the now-barren roots were ripped from the ground. These roots were rolled and twisted into wreaths, embellished with dried flowers, and hung on the door of the house to symbolize the cyclical nature of the seasons. The garden will lie fallow through the Winter while the Earth regenerates Her energy. In the seasonal circle, everything returns to life in Spring.

Many customs were observed. The plants were personified as Corn Mother, Wheat Woman, Lady Rye, and Harvest Queen; and Her consort was the Green Man, the Grain King, the Sun-Father. People approached the Harvest with deep solemnity and joyous celebration. To emphasize Continuous Creation, soil or seed from this year's harvest was often kept through the Winter and mixed with the Spring planting.

This practice also reflected a belief about human existence: that the *body,* like the husk of the corn, dies and falls away but the *spirit,* like the seed, is reborn in the Spring of Existence. Beliefs such as this were held by the original people of North America and by the Europeans and Africans who came to this land. The Harvest Home celebration was eco-spiritual, *not* political.

According to American history, President George Washington named the last Thursday in November as a National Thanksgiving

Day in 1789. The story of how the pilgrims learned to catch, plant, harvest, and cook "New World" foods under the instruction of the Native people became romanticized. The holiday was further institutionalized in 1861 when the slave states seceded and the Civil War started.

> During the worst of the fighting, President Lincoln in an attempt to bolster unionist spirit appointed the last Thursday in November as an annual National thanksgiving holiday. Soon afterwards, the northern regions won the war and the union was preserved. . . . The tradition of a combined harvest home, and thanksgiving day feast celebrated nationally was accepted. The "new" holiday featured all the characteristics common today.[41]

Today Thanksgiving is celebrated primarily by feasting on a Native American meal. The menu is: roast turkey, cornbread dressing, cranberry sauce, and pumpkin pie and democracy (a gift from the Native people). Some people build bonfires or light candles. Others hold processions or attend department store parades. Still others go to church or tumble with their children in the leaves. But everyone is basking in the sense of security that comes from a warm home and good food, while outside change whistles in the wind.

Black Friday

As stated earlier, I have long been aggravated by the crass commercialism of the latter part of the year. We manage to have fun on Halloween, enjoy a quiet moment with family and friends on

Thanksgiving, and then the Great Christmas rush is upon us. Cohen and Coffin, in *America Celebrates,* have explained the significance of Black Friday, the day after Thanksgiving.

Since World War II Black Friday has marked the beginning of the Christmas shopping campaign. American business considers this day auspicious and regards it as "a consumer bellwether that accurately forecasts the economy's climate as a whole."[42] Merchants count on the Christmas shopping frenzy to get out of "the red" (debt, economic uncertainty) and into "the black" (profit), thereby giving Black Friday a positive connotation (from their point of view).

Once more the connection between the fertility of the Earth (the Goddess), the harvest (gross national product), and wealth (economic security) is demonstrated. In most cultures both religious and civic festivals are accompanied by trade fairs and the sale of food.

Oya rules the Marketplace, the Cemetery, and Lightning. Shango, the Lord of Thunder and Fire, is Her husband. Together they are the tropical storm that uproots old structures, the rain that fertilizes the Earth, the great release of electrical energy that clears and cleans the atmosphere.

In the Western Hemisphere Shango is associated with a Catholic saint and is often referred to as Santa Bárbara Africana (in Spanish-speaking countries). This association is frequently misunderstood as He is also the God of Masculinity. It is not gender but natural force that these two share. In the Basque country (in Spain) Santa Bárbara is associated with storms and lightning. Traditionally her feast day is December 3 and Santa Bárbara Africana (Shango) is celebrated on December 4.

Oya is the Queen of the Marketplace and Her husband Shango is the CEO, associated with business acumen and benevolence.

"In Grenada, Shango Dances take place in the home of a queen and are given on such occasions as Thanksgiving at the end of the harvest, the consecration of a new house, payment for a vow, or requests for the power to intercede in a financial venture."[43] In Trinidad one of Shango's principal annual rituals is "feeding the children," an act of Thanksgiving.

In this time of homelessness and hunger I want to share a personal experience.

In the chapter on Winter I wrote of attending an Olokun ceremony in Benin and "swallowing the Moon." My hair was braided in the style of Shango devotees. At that ceremony the medium said to me, "Shango say that if you take care of the children, your name will be known all over the world." Before that trip to Africa, I had not done any long-distance or international travel beyond Canada, Hawaii, and Mexico. Since I began following Shango's directive, I have been invited to Europe, South America, Indonesia, and Australia, and everywhere I go, at least part of my time is spent with the children—whether at a hospital, a puppet show, or on the beach. I am always renewed by the presence of the children and I am always reminded that *children are life after death*. I highly recommend that you incorporate the feeding of hungry children into your spiritual practice; it will bring you joy and a surprising luck dynamic.

·‿ *The Autumn Rituals* ·‿

The Autumn Equinox Altar

The Autumn rituals celebrate the cyclical connection between the abundance of the harvest and the gifts of the ancestors. This connection can be beautifully illustrated by building an Ancestral Harvest altar.

Choose the site of the altar according to the structure of your home. You may want to build it outside in the garden area, on the deck or porch, or in the kitchen or dining room. If you have prepared and maintained a ritual room (as described in the chapter on 'Winter), then you may want to dress your North altar for this occasion.

For this altar you will need:

1. An image of the Dark Goddess. You may use a statue, a doll, a mask, or a figure made from twisted roots. As a really nice touch, use a shiny fat eggplant to represent the Goddess.

2. Nine glasses of water. They may be regular drinking glasses or chalices. They may be glass or ceramic. If you prefer metal, use copper.

3. Images of the ancestors. These may be photographs, dolls, sugar skulls, or personal effects.

4. Four seven-day candles in glasses. Use brown, orange, green, and yellow candles.

5. An assortment of vegetation representative of the season. For example: Fall leaves, Chinese lantern, pumpkin, squash, gourd, corn, buckeye, nuts.

6. A spirited liquid: burgundy, plum wine, or cranberry juice.

7. Nine pinwheels.

8. A piece of decorative seasonal fabric.

9. A bowl of grain and coins.

Building the Altar

Cover the altar area with the seasonal fabric. Seasonal fabric may be any earthy color. Some stores sell Halloween and harvest prints that feature landscapes of pumpkins, leaves, and other appropriate images, or you may use a solid color. If this altar is being built in the garden, you may want to use a piece of board or ceramic tile to establish your space. Or you may mark the bare earth by drawing a circle in the soil. Another meaningful way to establish the foundation of this altar is to take the dried roots from your garden and twist them together, fasten with cloth or wire into a wreath, and place the wreath on the altar. The wreath is also nice for the indoor altar.

I have a wreath made of Georgia kudzu root that will last for a long time. Kudzu was imported from Japan and now runs rampant in the southern United States. All efforts to control it only result in increased growth. Ivy vine (the resurrection plant) is another good wreath plant. Make sure your wreath is large enough to accommodate all altar objects.

Placing the Goddess

Place the image of the Dark Goddess (B) in the center of this wreath (A). Appropriate images would be Oya (you can use the eggplant) or one of Her Catholic equivalents (St. Theresa, St. Joan of Arc, Our Lady of Candelaria, etc.). Or you may want to use Madam Pele of Hawaii, Hecate of the Greeks, Kali-Ma of India, or some other brave and fierce woman image.

As you place Her in the center, declare that She is the "Boss Lady of the Marketplace, the Harvest, and the Cemetery."

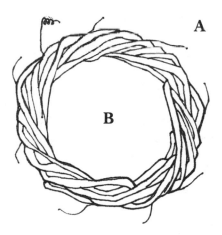

Placing the Souls

Next you will place the glasses of water for the nine layers of the soul. Place them in this order:

1. *The Universal Soul:* Place the Universal Soul in the
   North point of the circle.
2. *The Astral Soul:* Place the Astral Soul in the East point
   of the circle.

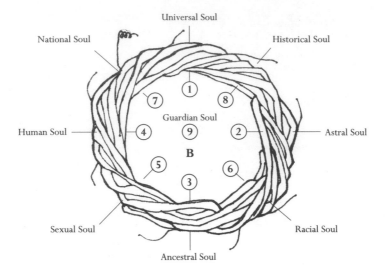

3. *The Ancestral Soul:* Place the Ancestral Soul in the South point of the circle.

4. *The Human Soul:* Place the Human Soul in the West point of the circle.

5. *The Sexual Soul:* Place the Sexual Soul in the Southwest point of the circle.

6. *The Racial Soul:* Place the Racial Soul in the Southeast point of the circle.

7. *The National Soul:* Place the National Soul in the Northwest point of the circle.

8. *The Historical Soul:* Place the Historical Soul in the Northeast point of the circle.

9. *The Guardian Soul:* The glass representing the Guardian Soul should be placed in the center behind the image of the Goddess. For this altar She is the Guardian of the harvest, the ancestors, and the souls.

Placing the Candles

Place the candles in the four directions with the Goddess figure and Her water glasses as their center. I recommend this layout for the candles:

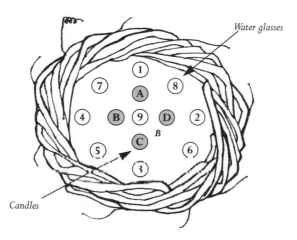

Water glasses

Candles

1. *A. Brown Candle:* Place the brown candle in the North to represent the dark Earth at rest after the harvest.

2. *B. Yellow Candle:* Place the yellow candle in the East to represent the intelligence and potential contained in the seed as it lies in the generative Earth.

3. *C. Orange Candle:* Place the orange candle in the South to represent the power and strength that the plant receives from the energy of the Sun.

4. *D. Green Candle:* Place the green candle in the West to represent the plant grown and yielding forth its nourishment.

Placing the Ancestors

Next we will place the photographs and personal possessions of the ancestors in the inner circle (around the Goddess, between the candles). In placing these images you may follow your intuition or the guidelines below.

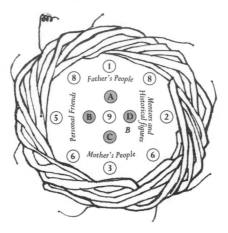

1. Place the images of *Father's people* in the North point of the circle to represent Father Sky.
2. Place the images of *Mother's people* in the South point to represent Mother Earth.
3. Place the images of *mentors and historical figures* in the East point to represent our intellectual and creative inheritance.
4. Place the images of *personal friends* in the West point to represent emotional and communal inheritance.

Placing the Harvest

Feel free now to place the leaves, gourds, roots, and flowers, the symbols of the harvest, wherever you like inside the wreath. Yes, this may include animals and rocks.

Consecration of the Shrine

You may now consecrate your shrine. To do this, first sprinkle it with a mixture of grain and money. Share breath with the mixture. Inhale its essence and send forth your breath; then toss this mixture up in the air and let it fall where it may. Second, anoint the altar with wine or juice by pouring three drops directly on the image of the Goddess and at the four gateways of the Sacred Circle. These liquids may represent both the blood of the Goddess and the semen of the Sun-King. Third, light the candles, beginning at the North and moving East, South, and West, while invoking the power of Autumn. You may use the Oriki Oya at the beginning of this chapter or a standard harvest prayer from another tradition. You may also sing a song or merely speak to the attributes of the season.

Using the Shrine: I recommend building this altar on or about September 21 and allowing it to remain until December 20. Once built, it becomes the place to meditate, communicate with ancestors, and concentrate on Abundance during the Fall season. This is the place to perform abundance rituals such as "pouring money,"[44] to design your prosperity plans, and to voice your concerns about homelessness, world hunger, and the failing economy.

The power of this altar is enhanced by vegetables from your garden or objects made with your own hands. During meditation at this altar, always remember the cycle of birth, growth, death, and rebirth as a dynamic operating in Nature and in your communal and personal affairs.

Placing the Pinwheels

Wind is the dominant generating force in Autumn. You may want to witness Oya's power by placing nine pinwheels around your yard, on the outside of your house, or near the windows inside your apartment. They will serve to remind you of the visible effects (spinning of the wheel) of the invisible force (the wind). They also generate electrical energy and blow away stagnation through currents of moving air. Indoors, this can be enhanced by using a spicy potpourri—my favorite is cinnamon, vanilla, and amaretto.

The Days of the Dead

In my spiritual family we perform rituals for Oya and the Egungun from October 18 to November 2. Usually the weekend bridging October 31 (Hallomas), November 1 (the Feast of All Saints), and November 2 (All Souls' Day) features the most elaborate rituals of the season.

At this time we test the progress of the mediums in training by conducting an *IkuNjoko*. IkuNjoko is a ceremony in which the spirits of benevolent ancestors are invited to "come sit down" in the body and consciousness of trained mediums. Those who have studied, meditated, and completed other rituals now channel the Intelligence of the ancestors. At this ceremony the ancestors speak, advising family members on right action and foretelling events to come.

We also hold a modern *Masquerade Egungun*. This is the drama of the ancestors. Each person chooses a member of the family or other revered personage, researches the life of that individual, and writes a biographical narrative. The person masquerades in the clothing, body paint, voice, and personality of the ancestor and performs the biographical sketch in the *first person* ("I" rather than "she").

The masquerader attempts to re-create not only the actions but also the attitudes and emotions of that particular ancestor. The audience is allowed to question the actors/ancestors about their lives and times.

This masquerade is modern. It differs from the traditional African masquerade in that the identity of the actors is known to all. But like the African ceremony, this sacred theater may go on for three or more days.

Another modern practice is that of delivering an *Ancestral Journey report*. This is a report on the history and practices of the participant's *mother culture*. Usually it focuses on the belief system (concepts of life, death, and the afterlife) and the funeral and ancestor reverence practices in that culture. The participant must do some research, acquire or make artifacts, write a paper, and present the material to the extended family.

Time and energy must be invested in discerning the appropriate culture to study. The United States is composed of Native people and Imported people from many countries and cultures. Some of us cannot trace our lineage directly. An intelligent guess must be made and some effort exerted to expand our knowledge.

I recommend that three kinds of Ancestral Journey reports be considered: reports on the mother culture, reports on an affinity culture, and human-family reports.

The Mother Culture: A culture from one's general racial and geographical background should be given first priority: Africa for African Americans, Asia for Asian Americans, and Europe for Euro-Americans. Children of mixed ancestry may report on the culture of either or both parents.

An Affinity Culture: An affinity culture is one that the participant is naturally attracted to and/or has studied and participated in. For example, many Euro-Americans are attracted to Native American or East Indian spirituality. The Affinity Culture report is a way of acknowledging the wisdom of these traditions and respectfully giving credit where it is due.

In my opinion, an Affinity Culture report should be done only *after* one has explored and presented a report on the Mother Culture (and preferably from pre-Christian, premonotheistic times). In this way, each person must acknowledge the gifts and limitations chosen by the Racial and Ancestral Soul layers. It stops people from escaping into a false identity, from becoming "wanna-be's" or "culture vultures." It also helps one to overcome the internalized oppression known as self-hatred. Then the Affinity Culture report becomes a labor of honor, not an exercise in cultural appropriation.

The Human Family: Now we must commit a great act: we must attempt to understand that which repulses us. In the Human Family report, participants are asked to pinpoint the people/culture that they dislike the most. This brings up ethnocentrism (the Irish and the English), religious imperialism (Moslems and Christians), and racism (the White and Black world).

Not only must the participant learn the beliefs, gifts, and limitations of that group; she must also find the common chords of humanity between her culture and the "alien other." This is often a hard thing to do. But striving to achieve it is a step in the direction of cleansing the National, Historical, Racial, and Ancestral layers of the soul and elevating the Human Soul—bringing it into closer proximity with the Universal Soul.

For those who take their ancestor reverence and spiritual study seriously, I highly recommend working on these three reports.

Sweeping the Cemetery

It is an old New Orleans custom to wash, paint (white), and decorate the vaults (built above ground) in the cemetery. Sometimes family members will light candles, bring food, and have a picnic with loved ones in the cemetery.

One of the most important rituals my family performs is that of sweeping the cemetery and attending neglected graves. If your family wishes, you may perform a similar ritual.

For this ritual you will need the following things. Take all of them to the cemetery with you.

1. a broom
2. nine pennies
3. a large bouquet of flowers
4. a white candle (in a glass)
5. a garbage bag
6. a jar of salt water
7. a hand towel

The Broom: Before you leave your house, take a regular household broom and decorate it with nine strips of ribbon of different colors. Fasten the ribbons to the whisk part of the broom. Sprinkle or spray the broom with rum or other spirits. This broom goes to the cemetery with you.

215

Entering the Cemetery: As you approach the gateway of the cemetery, knock three times, asking the gatekeeper for permission to enter. You may address the gatekeeper as Elegba, as Ghede-Nibo, as St. Peter, or simply as "the gatekeeper." When you feel you have permission, turn around in a circle, scraping your feet against the ground as if cleaning your shoes. Then face the gate and throw three pennies over the threshold of the gate. Step in.

Finding Your Territory: Most cemeteries have a paupers' or John Doe section where poor people or those who were buried free are deposited. Or you may simply look for a neglected area. Determine that you will establish a starting place by placing the white candle on the ground at that spot. Light the candle and speak to the spirits in that area. State your name and your intention, making it clear that you are not a thief and that you have come to "settle the stirring."

Sweeping the Cemetery: Now use your broom to sweep the graveyard. Pick up dead flowers, bottles, cans, and other debris and place them in the garbage bag. Sweep smaller particles away from the gravestones; clear paths and tidy up walkways. Avoid sweeping anyone's feet, including your own.

Placing the Flowers: Now lay a few flowers on as many graves as you've cleaned in that area. If the headstones have names, pronounce the names of the ancestors. As you lay the flower down, say, "Mojuba, love and respect to you, Ms. Mary Jones." If you have the urge to talk, do so. If you have the urge to listen, do so. Shake out the broom. Throw the garbage bag in a receptacle inside the cemetery, or the nearest receptacle outside the cemetery. If it is safe (in a glass), leave the candle burning; otherwise, snuff it out with wet fingers and burn the candle at home on your ancestor shrine. Gather up yourself and your things. As you leave this area, throw three pennies behind you.

Leaving the Cemetery: As you approach the gate (please leave by the same gate you entered), stop on the graveyard side of the threshold. Open the jar of salt water. Wet your hands, sprinkle the water around yourself, clean your aura by sprinkling water over your entire body, starting at the top of your head, and spilling some on your shoes. Dry your hands. Face the cemetery and ask the spirits to let there be peace and tranquility in the neighborhood. Step over the threshold. Throw the last three pennies over your left shoulder. Walk away and don't look back.

A Feast of Bread and Souls

In addition to the feasting done at Thanksgiving, November and December lend themselves to a number of small but endearing acts. Here are four recommendations:

1. Feeding Hungry Children: In this time of great homelessness, there is no ritual more pleasing to Shango than feeding hungry children. It doesn't call for a lot of fanfare or money. Just cook whatever you have in abundance or can get in quantity cheaply. Cook and serve. You may prepare individual packets of food (vegetable pies) or lay a blanket in the park and set a table of rice, beans, bread, and salad. My family has done this on several occasions and the people are always accepting, warm, and friendly.

Although you could make a monetary contribution to a food project or shelter, it has always been important to me to cook and serve with my own hands.

2. Moon Bathing: Catch the reflection of the Full Moon in a bowl of water, then take a bath in that water while asking for prosperity and the blessing of the ancestors. Of course the Harvest Moon is really nice for this ritual, but it can be done at any Full Moon of the year.

3. Crown of the Sunset: Take an old hat and decorate it with Autumn leaves. Sew or glue them onto the hat, or simply stick them in the hatband, and wear your crown with joy.

4. The Dumb Supper: The group cooks a meal consisting of food from your respective ancestral cultures. All the cooking is done in *total silence.* A table is set with a place setting for each human participating. There is a special place setting in the *center* of the table. This plate contains dirt from the cemetery with a white candle in its center. Participants bless the food (at 11:55 P.M.), place a little of each dish on the central plate, then leave the room and do not return until 12:05 A.M. This gives the spirits the opportunity to eat first. When the humans return they may eat in silence. At meal's end the contents of the central plate may be placed on the ancestor shrine, left in the cemetery, or put in the compost.

⌣·

In this work we have danced through the seasons—Winter, Spring, Summer, and Autumn. We've concentrated on the equinoxes and solstices as the major transitions. We have masqueraded in the African bush, celebrated on the beaches of Brazil, and meditated quietly in our homes and neighborhoods.

While these holidays are important and should be marked with great celebration, so should you know that every day is a holy day. And we, the children of Earth, should praise and celebrate the New Moon and the Full Moon, Sunrise and Sunset. We must awaken every morning and retire each night knowing that we are the children of Natural Force, that we are part of the never-ending cycle of the seasons of life, and that every day we can celebrate in a Carnival of the Spirit.

Luisah Teish, womanchief
September 22, 1993, 6:28 P.M.

Notes

1. The Rev. Samuel Johnson, ed., *The History of the Yorubas: From the Earliest Times to the Beginning of the British Protectorate* (Westport, CT: Negro Univ. Press, 1970), 26.

2. Melville J. Herskovits, *Dahomey: An Ancient West African Kingdom,* 2 vols. (Evanston, IL: Northwestern Univ. Press, 1967), 2:101–3.

3. A. B. Ellis, *The Yoruba Speaking People of the Slave Coast of West Africa* (Chicago: Benin Press, 1964), 45.

4. Lawrence Durdin-Robertson, *The Year of the Goddess: A Perpetual Calendar of Festivals* (Northamptonshire, England: Aquarius Press, 1990), 197.

5. Alice van Straalen, *The Book of Holidays Around the World* (New York: Dutton, 1986), 159.

6. Marion Green, *A Calendar of Festivals*: Traditional Celebrations, Songs, Seasonal Recipes, and Things to Make (Rockport, MA: Element, Inc., 1991), 133.

7. Gert Chessi, *Voodoo: Africa's Secret Power* (Austria: Perlinger Verlag, 1979), 253.

8. Chessi, *Voodoo,* 147.

9. Chessi, *Voodoo,* 148.

10. Alfred Metraux, *Voodoo in Haiti* (New York: Schocken, 1972).

11. Ulli Beier, ed., *Yoruba Poetry: Anthology of Traditional Power* (Cambridge Univ. Press, 1970), 33.

12. John G. Jackson, *Introduction to African Civilization* (Secaucus, NJ: Citadel Press, 1970), 56, quoting Archibald Robinson, *Morals in World History* (London: Watts & Co., 1945), 21–22.

13. Jackson, *Introduction to African Civilization,* 56.

14. Lyle Saxon, Robert Tallant, and Edward Dreyer, *Gumbo YaYa: Collection of Louisiana Folktales.* (New York: Bonanza, 1945), 19.

15. Saxon, *Gumbo Ya Ya,* 3.

16. Saxon, *Gumbo Ya Ya,* 19.

17. Riane Eisler, *The Chalice and the Blade: Our History, Our Future* (San Francisco: Harper & Row, 1987), 102.

18. Barbara G. Walker, *The Woman's Encyclopedia of Myths and Secrets* (San Francisco: Harper & Row, 1983), 267.

19. Priscilla Sawyer Lord and Daniel J. Foley, *Easter the World Over* (Philadelphia: Chilton, 1971), 212–13.

20. Lord and Foley, *Easter the World Over,* 203–4.

21. Harold Courlander, *A Treasury of Afro-American Folklore: The Oral Literature, Tradition, Recollections, Legends, Songs, Religious Beliefs, Customs, Sayings, and Humor of Peoples of African Descent in the Americas.* (New York: Crown, 1976), 61–62.

22. Geoffrey Parrinder, *African Mythology* (New York: Harper & Row, 1986), 67.

23. Monica Sjoo and Barbara Mor, *The Great Cosmic Mother: Rediscovering the Religion of the Earth* (San Francisco: Harper & Row, 1987), 253.

24. Sjoo and Mor, *Great Cosmic Mother,* 254.

25. Parrinder, *African Mythology,* 27.

26. Melville Herskovits, *Dahomean Narrative* (Evanston, IL: Northwestern Univ. Press, 1958) 159–62.

27. Geraldine Thorster, *God Herself: The Female Roots of Astrology* (New York: Avon, 1981), 100.

28. Herbert Thurston and Donald Attwater, eds., *Butler's Lives of the Saints* (New York: Kennedy, 1956), 631–32.

29. Thurston and Attwater, *Butler's Lives,* 632.

30. Merlin Stone, *Ancient Mirrors of Womanhood: Our Goddess and Heroine Heritage,* 2 vols. (New York: New Sibylline Books, 1979), 2:78.

31. Murry Hope, *The Way of Cartouche* (New York: St. Martin's Press, 1985), 69–70.

32. Zora Neale Hurston, *Of Mules and Men* (Philadelphia: Lippincott, 1935), 202.

33. Tallant, *Gumbo Ya Ya*, 429.

34. Hennig Cohen and Tristran Potter Coffin, *America Celebrates!: A Patchwork of Weird and Wonderful Holiday Lore* (Detroit: Visible Ink Press, 1991), 209.

35. P. Mercier, "The Fon of Dahomey," in *African Worlds: Studies in the Cosmological Ideas and Social Values of African Peoples,* ed. Daryll Forde (London: Oxford Univ. Press, 1954), 220.

36. John S. Mbiti, *The Prayers of African Religion* (Maryknoll, NY: Orbis Books, 1975), 106.

37. See Luisah Teish, *Jambalaya: The Natural Woman's Book of Personal Charms and Practical Rituals* (San Francisco: Harper & Row, 1985), chapter 8.

38. Joseph Campbell, *Oriental Mythology: The Masks of God* (New York: Penguin, 1962), 58–59.

39. Murry Hope, *Practical Egyptian Magic* (New York: St. Martin's Press 1984), 57.

40. Awo Falokun Fatunmbi, *Iwa Pele, Ifa Quest: The Search for the Source of Santeria and Lucumi* (New York: Original Pub., 1991), 41–42.

41. Cohen and Coffin, *America Celebrates,* 305–6.

42. Cohen and Coffin, *America Celebrates,* 330.

43. G. E. Simpson, *Black Religions in the New World* (New York: Columbia Univ. Press, 1978), 83.

44. Teish, *Jambalaya,* 35–36.

Index

Abiku, 198–99
Ache (Power), 173–74
Aestras, 117
Affinity culture report, 213
Africa, xiii, 169–70; and astrology,
    154–55; bush, 197; Egungun mas-
    querade, 213; and elephant, 86;
    Royal Barge, 86; slave trade, xii–xiii,
    141–42; Yemonja, 25. *See also*
    African diaspora; Algeria; Angola;
    South Africa; Trinidad; West Africa;
    Zimbabwe
African Americans, xiii; Independence
    Day, 114, 135–36; Kwanzaa, 35; and
    Mardi Gras, 84–88. *See also* African
    diaspora; Slavery
African diaspora, xiii, 39, 123; beliefs,
    169–70; creation myths, 11–20;
    grounds blessings, 98; Oshun Queen
    of, 79; Water Spirits, 39–43; Yam
    Festival, 164; Yemonja in, 25. *See also*
    Black people; Deities; Divination;
    New Orleans; Rituals
Aganju, 25
Agwe Taroyo, 39, 42–43
Aina, 148
Air, invocation to, 153
Aje, of West Africa, 197–98

Akewa, 124
Akwambo, 117
Aladora, Iyal'Orisha Omi, 175
Algeria, Ibeji Ceremony, 115
Al-llat, 123
All Saints' Day, 119, 212
All Souls' Day, 119, 168, 212
Altars: Autumn Equinox, 205–12; build-
    ing, 55–58; consecration, 211
Amaterasu, 116, 124
America Celebrates (Cohen & Coffin), 203
Amsterdam, 36–37
Ancestor Reverence Day, 115
Ancestors: in Autumn rituals, 189–93,
    194–95, 205, 210, 212–15; deifi-
    cation of, 184–93; ghosts and,
    183–84; Halloween and, 167,
    194–95; litany of, 189–93; rebirth
    of, 173; reverence for, 100–103,
    115, 168, 180–94, 215; spirits of,
    180–84; in Spring rituals, 81, 87,
    100–103
Ancestral Journey report, 213–14
Ancestral Soul, 178, 208, 214
Angola, Nzinga of, 191–93
Animals, 127; Blessing of, 112; sacrifice of
    (substitutes), 98; souls, 185; World
    Day for, 118

225

Anointing, in rituals, 66
Antelope Boy, Marriage of Snake Maiden
    with, 117
Anyanwu, 124
Apache: Painted Woman, 78; Sunrise
    Dance, 117, 162
Aphrodite, 78
April, 114–15; April showers face wash,
    110–11
Aquarius, 157
Arabia, Attar/Al-llat, 123
Argentina: Akewa, 124; Carnival, 95–96
Aries, 93, 112, 154, 157; invocation to,
    153
Ashanti people, on map, 16
Ash Wednesday, 112
Asia: Amaterasu, 116, 124; Kwan yin,
    115. *See also individual countries*
Astral Soul, 177, 185, 207
Astrology, 154–55, 157. *See also individual
    signs and deities*
Attar, 123
August, 116–17
Authentic tales, repeated/returned,
    xiv–xv, 26–27
Autumn, 118–19, 159–219; deities,
    160–62, 203–4; Equinox, 33, 118,
    145, 146, 163, 205–12; harvest,
    162–64, 200–202, 205, 210; rituals,
    162–67, 184, 187–88, 194–96,
    205–19
Aztecs, Coaticue, 161

Babylonia, Ishtar, 113
Bacchanalia, 82
Bali, Women's Fertility Day, 115
Bath: first rain in May, 103–11; moon,
    218; pre-ritual, 58
Bean Throwing Festival, 113
Belgium: palm tree rituals, 94; Shrimp
    Festival, 117
Bembe Ngoma, 142–43
Benin: dream, 43–46; Gelede, 198
Big Bang, 13, 50, 176
Birth, 172–74
Birthday of the Sun, 116
Black Codes, xiii, 143
Black Friday, 118, 202–4
Black History Month, 113

Black Indians, 87
Black Madonna, 117, 162; Feast of, 116
Black people: and Mardi Gras, 84–89;
    pasabonne, 88–89; "pride and aware-
    ness," 8; and sanctity of food, 167.
    See also Africa; African Americans
Black Peter, 37–38
Blessing: altar cloth, 53; grounds, 97–103
Blessing of the Animals, 112
Blue Mother Moon, 23–24
Bobo Masquerade, 115
Bona Dea, 115
Bonnet, Easter, 92–93
Brazil: Candelaria, 116; Carnivals, 95;
    Celebration of Twins, 113, 119;
    deities, 25, 30, 39, 41, 112; Gelede,
    198; and Nzinga, 193
Bride of Summer, 117, 139–41
Broken Doll Day, 114
Brooms: for cemetery sweeping, 215–16;
    for ritual room cleaning, 53–54
Bull Running, 116
Burkina Faso, Bobo Masquerade, 115
Burning of the Lamps, 116
Bush of Ghosts, 197–200

Cable, George Washington, 145
Calendar, 112–19; Egyptian, 129, 138–39;
    Gede, 155; Western Sun-oriented, xiv
Calinda dance, 144
Cancer, 154, 157; invocation to, 153; Sun
    in, 134, 145, 146
Candelaria, 116
Candlemas, 113
Candles: altar, 53–54; on Autumn Equinox
    altar, 209; planets associated with
    colors of, 156
Capistrano, swallows depart, 113, 119
Capoeira, 193
Capricorn, 112, 154, 157; invocation to,
    153; Saturnalia and, 34
Caribbean Islands: Carnival, 95; Yam Festi-
    val, 117, 163; Yemonja, 25. *See also*
    Cuba; Haiti; Jamaica
Carnival, 82–88, 95–96, 112
Catholicism, 88, 127–28; canonization in,
    193; church celebrations, 6–7; and
    death days of saints, 136; Mardi Gras,
    82–83, 84; in New Orleans, 84,

141; Oshun in, 79–80; Santa Bárbara Africana, 203; and slave trade, xiii; Visitation of Our Lady, 137. *See also* Christmas; Easter

Celts, Sunna, 124

Cemetery, sweeping, 215–17

Chaka, 193

Changing Woman, 161, 162

Character, development of, 180, 181–82

Chessi, Gert, 40–41

Children, feeding hungry, 204, 218

China: Feast of the Lanterns, 112; Hungry Ghost Festival, 117; Kite Flying, 113, 119; Midautumn Festival, 117, 163; mooncakes, 117, 163; Qing Ming, 115

Chinese New Year, 112, 113

Christianity, xiii, 91; church celebrations, 6–7; Heaven, 170; June bride, 140; Light Celebrations, 34, 35; and Mardi Gras, 84; and Principle of Renewal, 82; St. John's Day, 141; Sanctified church, 127–28. *See also* Catholicism; Christmas; Easter; Jesus; John the Baptist; Mary Christmas, 2–4, 30, 62; Black Friday and, 203; at church, 6–7; European, 34, 36–38; gifts, 5–6; and Winter Solstice, 33, 34, 35

Clothing: in African rituals, 42; Easter, 92–93; as gifts, 5–6; ripped for New Year, 69; Zulu Parade, 85

Coaticue, 161

Cochon Gris, 119–20

Cocomama, 78

Coffin, Tristran Potter, 203

Cohen, Hennig, 203

Composite tales, xv, 11–12

Corn and Flag Dance, 115

Corn Goddess, 117

Corn rituals, Native American, 115, 116, 164

Costa Rica, Feast of the Black Madonna, 116

Cow Festival, 113

Creation, 11–20, 125–26, 171; Big Bang, 13, 50, 176; Continuous, 172, 201; "First Cause," 18; images, 92

Crown of the Sunset, 218

Cuba: deities, 39, 41–42; Feast of Shango, 118; Feast of the Mother of Mercy, 118; Feast of Yemaya and Oshun, 116, 162; palm tree rituals, 94

Cure Salé, 116, 162

Curses, family, 178

Dahomey: ancestor deification, 186; fire quest, 134; map, 16. *See also* Fon people

Damballah Aida Hwedo, 126, 171–72

Dark Goddess, Autumn Equinox altar, 206, 207

Daughter of Promise, 75–76, 108, 115. *See also* Oshun

Daughters of the Gelefun, 30–32

Davis, Wade, 196

Dead, Days of, 212–15. *See also* All Saints' Day; All Souls' Day; Hallomas/Halloween

Death, 172–74; rituals, 186–87

December, 112–13, 118–19

Deer Mother Dance, 112

Deification process, 185–93

Deities, 15–20; ancestors, 184–93; astrological, 157; Autumn, 160–62, 203–4; planets associated with, 157; Spring, 76–82; Summer, 122–25, 129, 134–35, 138–39; Winter, 25–26, 39–43, 48–51. *See also* individual deities

Depression, rainwater lifting, 110–11

Día de los Muertos, 9, 119, 168, 195

Dick and Jane, 164–65

Dilloggun, 13, 42

Directions: altar, 56–58; invocations to, 58–60, 99–100, 147–50, 153–54; working, 148–50

Divination, 13, 19–20, 42, 48–49; and ancestor deification, 187–88; destiny-directed/will-directed, 48; and family spirit, 180; New Year, 72

Dogon people: ancestor deification, 186; fire quest, 133–34; on map, 16

Dolls, 6; Broken Doll Day, 114

Dream chart, New Year, 68–69, 70–72

Dreams, 42, 46; Benin, 43–46; Mermaid, 42

Du, 19–20

Dumb Supper, 218–19
Duppies, 199

Earth, 126–27; invocation to, 153
Earth Day, 115
Easter, 6–7, 82, 88, 90–91, 114
Ebbo, 72n
Egbe Egungun, 186–88, 190–91; mas-
  querade, 187–88, 194–95, 212–13
Egg: cosmogenetic/Easter, 92–93; in
  Spring rituals, 92–93, 104–5,
  109–10
Egypt, xiii, 8, 127–30; ancestor deifica-
  tion, 185–86; Breaking of the Nile,
  117; calendar, 129, 138–39; Dynastic
  Era, 129–30; Fire Ceremony, 117,
  162; Hathor, 78, 90, 115, 123, 134;
  Horus, 139, 186; lion, 134–35, 139;
  Nepthys, 116, 139, 161, 162; New
  Year, 116; Night of the Drop, 115;
  Pharaohs, 129, 186; Saleclo, Cresting
  the Nile, 113, 119; Sekhmet,
  134–35; Sirius, 115, 139. *See also*
  Isis; Osiris
Eleda, 16, 18, 19
Elegba, 48–51, 79, 112; Trickster-
  Magician/Linguist/Enforcer, 49–50
Elephant, 86; Dance, 117
Elizabeth (John's mother), 136–37
Emancipation Proclamation, 84, 135–36
Energy, and Matter, 13–14
England: Flurry Dance, 114; Mothering
  Sunday, 114; Mummers' Plays, 118
Eostre, 90, 112
Equinox: Autumn, 33, 118, 145, 146,
  163, 205–12; Spring, 33, 98–99,
  112, 114
Erzulie, 78
Eshu, 197
Europe: and Angola, 191–92; Christmas,
  34, 36–38; Halloween, 167; June
  brides, 139–40; palm tree rituals,
  94; pre-Christian, xiii; Santa Bárbara,
  203. *See also individual countries*
Everything Knowable, 16
Extrovert meditation, 72n
Eyo Masquerade, 117

Face painting, 85
Face wash, rainwater, 110–11

Fahamme Temple of Amun-Ra, St. Louis,
  8, 127–30, 167
Family: Ancestral Soul and, 178; of spirit,
  179–80. *See also* Ancestors
Father-God, 80–81, 125, 130
Fat Tuesday/Mardi Gras, 82–88, 112
February, 112–13
Feeding of the Springs, 117
Fertility: Carnival motif, 86, 87, 95;
  deities, 81–82; Easter symbols and,
  88, 93; Marawu Fertility Ritual, 118;
  Women's Fertility Day, 115
Fire: deities, 122–24; invocation to, 153;
  quest for, 133–35; rituals, 58–60,
  117, 162
Firewalk, 130–33
First Rain of May, 92
Floating Leaf Cups, Festival of, 119
Floralia, 114, 115
Flowers, in rituals, 114, 115, 152
Flurry Dance, 114
Fon people: ancestor deification, 186; cre-
  ation myth, 13; deities, 16–18; on
  map, 16
Food: boycotted, 4–5; Dumb Supper,
  218–19; Fat Tuesday, 82–83;
  grounds blessings ritual, 98; at Hallo-
  mas feasts, 195; for hungry children,
  204, 218; New Year's, 4; sanctity of,
  167; Thanksgiving and Christmas,
  3–4
Fortuna, Feast of, 114, 116
France: Festival of Mary Magdalene, 117;
  palm tree rituals, 94

Gaia hypothesis, 126–27
Ganesh, Festival of, 116, 162
Ganesha, Feast of, 116
Garland Day, 114
Gawai Payak, 115
Gede, 155
Gelede festival, 198
Gemini, 157
Gemstones, planets associated with, 156
Gender: gynophobia, 130; Sexual Soul
  choosing, 176. *See also* Patriarchies;
  Sexuality; Women
Ghana: Akwambo, 117; Homowo, 116;
  map, 16; Sasabonsam, 199; Yam
  Festival, 116, 163

228

Ghosts, 174, 183–84; Bush of, 197–200; Hungry Ghost Festival, 117
Gifts, Christmas, 5–6
Gods/Goddesses. *See* Deities
Good Friday, 115
Good Goddess, Feast of, 115
Grain King, 83, 86, 88, 91
Great Dance, 33
Great Mother, Feast of, 118
Greece: Aphrodite, 78; Feast of the Great Mother, 118; Hecate, 161, 207; Medusa, 161; Prometheus, 134
Green Corn Dance, 116
Green Man, Festival of, 115
Green Squash Festival, 113, 119
Grounds blessing, 97–103
Guardian Soul, 178–79, 208
Guatemala: Light Celebrations, 34–35; Rain Ceremony, 115
Gynophobia, 130

Haiti: Cochon Gris, 199–200; Damballah Hwedo realm, 171; deities, 30, 39, 42–43, 80, 122–23, 161; fear of becoming a zombie, 196; Ra-Ra Festival, 115; Saut d'Eau, 117
Hallomas/Halloween, 9, 118, 165–68, 183–84, 194–96, 200, 212
Hants, 199
Harvest, Autumn, 162–64, 200–202, 205, 210
Harvest Home, 200–202
Hathor, 78, 90, 115, 123, 134
Haumea, 78
Hawaiian Islands: Haumea, 78; Madam Pele, 127, 161, 207
Heaven, 170
Hecate, 161, 207; Festival of, 117
Heroism, fire and, 134
Hilaria, 113
Hinduism: Festival of Shiva, 119; Festival of Three Mothers, 118; Songs for Rain, 117. *See also* India
Historical Soul, 178, 208, 214
Hitler, Adolf, 194
Holland: and Angola, 192; Christmas, 36–38
Homowo, 116
Hooting at Hunger, 116

Hopi: Marawu Fertility Ritual, 118; Marriage of Snake Maiden and Antelope Boy, 117; Niman Kachina, 117; Snake Dance, 117
Horus, 139, 186
Human Family report, 213
Human Soul, 176, 185, 208, 214
Hungry Ghost Festival, 117

Ibae, 4n
Ibeji, 15; Ceremony, 115
Ibo people, xiii; Anyanwu, 124
Ibu Afo, 112
Iceland, Winter Nights, 118
Ides of March, 115
Ifa, 13, 16, 155
Ikoko Olokun, 29–30
IkuNjoko, 212
Ile Aiye, 126, 170–71, 174, 179–81, 183, 184
Ile Okun/Ile Olokun, 126, 170, 171, 174, 179–80, 183
Ile Orun, 126, 170, 171, 174, 179–81, 183, 184
Imani, 112
Imanje, 39, 41, 112
Inca, Birthday of the Sun, 116
Indara, 78
Independence Day: African American, 114, 135–36; Senegal, 114; Zimbabwe, 114
India: Feast of Ganesha, 116; Festival of Ganesh, 116, 162; Kali-Ma, 161, 207; Kali Puji, 118; Lakshmi Puji, 118; Laksmi, 78. *See also* Hinduism
Indombe, 124
Indonesia: Indara, 78; Women's Fertility Day, 115
Insanity, through negative influence, 182
International Literary Day, 116
International Women's Day, 9, 112
International Workers' Day, 115
Inuit, Sun Sister, 124
Invocations: to directions, 58–60, 99–100, 147–50, 153–54; to planets, 150–55
Ip'ori, 173
Iran, No Ruz, 114
Ireland, St. Brigid's Day, 113
Ishtar, 113

Isis, 129, 138–39, 141, 185; Light of, 116;
Marriage with Osiris, 116; Search
and Recovery of Osiris, 118
Islamic Ramadan, 115
Ix Chel, 78, 114
Iya Mapo, 14
Iyamis, 198

Jamaica, duppies, 199
January, 112–13
Japan: Amaterasu, 124; Bean Throwing
Festival, 113; Festival of the
Lanterns, 117; Lily Festival, 114,
135; Rice Festival, 114
Jazz, ancestors of, 87
Jesus, 90–91, 128, 137, 141; and ancestor
deification, 190; birth, 141; Cochon
Gris and, 200
John the Baptist, 136–39, 141. See also St.
John's Day
July, 116–17; Fourth of, 116
June, 114–17; brides, 139
Juneteenth, 9, 114, 135–36
Juno: Celebration, 112; Feast of Jupiter,
Juno, Minerva, 118
Jupiter: associations with, 156–57; Feast of
Jupiter, Juno, Minerva, 118; invoca-
tions to, 150–51

Kali-Ma, 161, 207
Kali Puji, 118
Karma, 174
King, Martin Luther, Jr., 112
King's Dance, 35, 112
Kite Flying, 113, 119
Kudzu, 206
Kuumba, 112
Kwan yin, 115
Kwanzaa, 9, 30, 35, 62–63, 112

Lady of the Sunset, 119, 160
Lakshmi Puji, 118
Laksmi, 78
Lammas, 116
Lanterns: Feast of, 112; Festival of, 117
LaVeau, Mam'zelle Marie, 143–44
Leap Year, 113
Lent, 82–83, 84, 88–90
Leo, 150, 157; Sun in, 134, 139, 145,
146

Libra, 154, 157, 163; invocation to, 153
Life, 172–74
Light Celebrations, 33–36
Light of Isis, 116
Lightning, 125
Lily Festival, 114, 135
Lincoln, Abraham, 202
Lion, 134–35, 139, 145
Lisa, 16–17, 18, 19
Lovedu, Rain Queen, 113, 119
Luciadagen, 34, 119

Malaysia, Gawai Payak, 115
Malcolm X, 115
Mali: map, 16; Tyi Wara, 114. See also
Dogon people
Maman Brigitte, 161
Mamissi, 40–42
Mami-Wata, 39–42, 112
Mandela, Nelson, freed, 112
Man on the Moon Day, 116
Marawu Fertility Ritual, 118
March, 112–15; Ides of, 113
Mardi Gras, New Orleans, 82–88, 112
Marriage of Isis and Osiris, 116
Marriage of Snake Maiden and Antelope
Boy, 117
Mars: associations with, 156–57; invoca-
tions to, 150–51
Mary, 79–80, 90–91, 124, 128, 137
Mary Magdalene, Festival of, 117
Masquerades: Bobo, 115; Egungun,
187–88, 194–96, 212–13; Eyo,
117
Matrilineal societies, mother-goddess,
80–81
Matronalia, 112
Matter: birth of, 19; and Energy, 13–14
Mawu, 16–17, 18, 19, 134; Day of, 119
May, 114–15; rain ritual, 103–11. See also
May Day
Maya: Ix Chel, 78, 114; New Year, 116;
nine layers of underworld, 175
May Day, 115, 139–40
Maypole Dance, 139–40
Meditation, extrovert, 72n
Memorial Day, 114
Mercury: associations with, 156–57; invo-
cation to, 153; and Virgo, 145–46
Mermaid, 39–42

Mexico: *posadas*, 34, 119; Tonantzin, 116; Virgen de Gaudalupe, 116, 119. *See also* Aztecs; Maya
Midautumn Festival, 117, 163
Midsommar, Festival of, 114, 136
Midsummer, rituals, 114, 136, 140–41, 143–44
Minerva, Feast of Jupiter, Juno, Minerva, 118
Monsters, 196–200
Moon, 123–25; associations with, 156–57; bath, 218; Blue Mother, 23–24; invocation to, 153; and Sun in Cancer, 145, 146
Mooncakes, 117, 163
Morning, designation of, 47
Mother culture report, 213
Mothering Sunday, 114
Mother of Mercy, Feast of, 118
Mother of the Night, 22–23, 113. *See also* Yemonja
Mother of the Sun, 138–39
Mothers, the, 34
Mother's Day, 9, 114
Mummers' plays, 38, 118
Myth, xiv; creation, 11–20, 125–26; Olokun, 26–27

Names: African, 9, 35; composer, 9; Luisah Teish, 129
Nana, 125
Nanabouclou, 122–23
Nana Buluku, 16–18
National Soul, 177–78, 186, 208, 214
Native Americans, xii–xiii, 93–96; Changing Woman, 161, 162; corn rituals, 115, 116, 164; fire quest, 134; Mardi Gras and, 87; and Thanksgiving, 202; and Turtle Island, 141. *See also* Apache; Aztecs; Hopi; Inca; Maya; Mexico; Pueblo
Natural Cycle, 33
Natural Forces, human behavior based on, 181–83, 184, 190
Nepal: Cow Festival, 113, 119; Lakshmi Puji, 118
Nepthys, 161, 162; Birth of, 116, 139
Neptune, associations with, 156–57
New Orleans, 141–42; Carnival/Mardi Gras, 82–88, 112; cemetery sweep-

ing, 215–16; Congo Square, 143; Gelede, 198; hants, 199; palm tree rituals, 95; schools, 88, 164–65; Summer, 142–45
New Year, 46–51; Chinese, 112, 113; Egypt, 116; Eve, 36; food, 4; Iran, 114; Mayan, 116; resolutions, 48; rituals, 36, 51, 67–72; Sierra Leone, 114
Niger: Cure Salé, 116, 162; map, 16
Nigeria: Benin City, 43; Eyo Masquerade, 117; Gelede, 198; Ile Ife, 48; map, 16; Noise Festival, 112; and Oshun, 79, 86. *See also* Ibo people; Yoruba people
Night of the Drop, 115
Niman Kachina, 117
Nine, numerologically, 175
"Nobody knows what's at the bottom of the ocean," 28–32
Noise Festival, 112
No Ruz, 114
November, 118–19
Numerology, 175
Nzinga, King of Ndongo, 191–93

Obatala, 14, 15, 25, 86
October, 118–19
Oduddua, 25
Odus, 13, 19–20, 42, 74, 182, 198
Oju Meta, 109
Okanran, 13, 50
"Old Folks Say" (Teish), 1–2
Olodumare, 16, 18, 19
Olokun, 26–32, 39, 42–46; predispositions from House of, 172; rituals, 29–32, 42–43, 62–67
Olorun, 16–17, 25, 79
Omitutu, 149
Onile, 149
Ops, Festival of, 112
Ori, 173–74, 179
Ori'bi, 182
Original tales, xv, 11–12, 74, 88–90, 142–43
Ori Inu, 173
Oriki, 67
"Oriki Oshun" (Teish), 75–76
"Oriki Oya" (Teish), 160
Orisha Idile, 190

Orisha Orile, 190
Orishas, 16, 190–91
Orungan, 25, 80n
Osa, 148, 182, 198
Oshun, xi–xii, xvi, 75–82, 86, 124; cry-
    ing, 111; Elegba and, 49; Feast of
    Yemaya and Oshun, 116, 162; names,
    78, 79–80; rituals, 106–7, 108, 116,
    162
Osiris, 129, 134, 139, 141; Marriage with
    Isis, 116; Search and Recovery by
    Isis, 118
Our Lady of Peace and Good Voyages, 115
Oya, 160–62, 197, 200, 203–4; Elegba
    and, 49; Hallomas and, 194–95;
    and negative Osa-condition, 182; and
    nine, 175; rituals for, 206, 212; and
    Shango, 189–90, 203–4
Oyotunji Village, South Carolina, 48, 175,
    178–79

Paganism, Light Celebrations, 34
Painted Woman, 78
Palm-product rituals, 93–96
Palm Sunday, 93, 115
Pasabonne, 88–89
Path Clearing, 117
Patriarchies: in Egypt, 129–30; father-god,
    80–81, 130; male Sun/female Earth,
    126; witches and, 197
Pele, Madam, 127, 161, 207
Perfection, 14–15
Peru: Cocomama, 78. *See also* Inca
Philippines, Our Lady of Peace and Good
    Voyages, 115
Pinwheels, on Autumn Equinox altar,
    211–12
Pisces, 157
Planets: associations with, 156–57; holi-
    days, 118; invocations to, 150–55.
    See also Moon; Saturn; Sun
Planter's Dance, 114
Plants, 127; for Autumn Equinox altar,
    206; souls, 185; winter, 52–53. *See
    also* Harvest
Ploughing Ceremony, 114
Pluto, associations with, 156–57
Political power, 133–35
Portuguese, and Angola, 191–92

Posadas, 34, 119
Power: Ache, 173–74; political, 133–35;
    Yemonja as, 32–33
Prometheus, 134
Ptah, 130
Pueblo: Corn and Flag Dance (New Mex-
    ico), 115; Deer Mother Dance, 112
Puerto Rico, palm tree rituals, 94

Qing Ming, 115
Quetzalcoatl, 116

Rabbit, Easter, 92–93
Racial Soul, 177, 208, 214
Racism, 130, 177
Rain, 125; rituals, 103–11, 115, 117
Rain Queen Lovedu, 113, 119
Ramadan, Islamic, 115
Ra-Ra Festival, 115
Reed, Aunt Marybelle, 4, 84
Reformation, The (personal holiday), 9
Reincarnation, 172–74
Renewal, Principle of, 82
Repeated tales, xiv–xv
Returned tales, xiv–xv, 26–27
Rex Parade, 83
Rice Festival, 114, 115
Ritual room, 52–54, 205
Rituals: Autumn, 162–67, 184, 187–88,
    194–96, 205–19; bath, 58, 103–11,
    218; cleansing fire, 60–62; clothing
    for, 42, 69; death, 186–87; and
    ghosts, 174, 184; palm-product,
    93–96; preparing for, 52–60; Spring,
    81, 82–88, 95–96, 97–111, 139–40;
    Summer, 135, 136, 140–41, 143–45,
    147–55; Winter, 29–32, 39–43,
    52–72, 112
River Goddess, Feast of, 118
Rome: Bacchanalia, 82; Bona Dea, 115;
    Day of Vesta, 115; Feast of Jupiter,
    Juno, Minerva, 118; Festival of Ops,
    112; Floralia, 114; Juno Celebration,
    112; Rosalia, 114; Saturnalia, 34;
    Saturnalion, 118
Rosalia/Rose Festival, 114

Sacred space, creating, 52–60
Sagittarius, 157

St. Anthony, 112
St. Brigid's Day, 113
St. Brigit, Feast of, 117
St. Clara's Day, 115
St. George's Day, 115
St. Joan of Arc, 114
St. John's Day, 116, 136–38, 141, 143–44
St. Joseph's Day, 91, 112
St. Lucia, Feast of, 118
St. Nicholas Day, 37–38, 118
St. Patrick's Day, 112
Saleclo, Cresting the Nile, 113, 119
Sanctified church, 127–28
Santa Bárbara Africana, 203
Santeria, xii
Sasabonsam, 199
Saturn: associations with, 156–57; invoca-
   tion to, 153; Saturnalia and, 34
Saturnalia, 34
Saturnalion, 118
Saut d'Eau, 117
Scent, planets associated with, 156
Scorpio, 157, 167
Sekhmet, 134–35; Feast of, 119
Seminole, Green Corn Dance, 116
Senegal: Independence Day, 114; map, 16
September, 116–19; rituals, 162–64
Seven African Principles, 35
Sexuality: Mermaid, 42; Oshun, 80;
   Spring ritual, 82, 106–7, 114; Sum-
   mer's erotic fulfillment, 139–41
Sexual Soul, 176, 208
Shango, 189–90, 203–4; Feast of, 118, 190
She-Elephant Dance, 117
Shiva, Festival of, 119
Shrimp Festival, 117
Sierra Leone: map, 16; New Year's Day,
   114
Sirius, 115, 139
Slavery, 145; Angola, 191–92; Black
   Codes, xiii, 143; and Carnival, 84;
   Emancipation Proclamation, 84,
   135–36; and family of spirit, 179–80;
   trade, xii–xiii, 25, 141–42
Snake Dance, 117
Snake Maiden, Marriage with Antelope
   Boy, 117
Solstice: Summer, 33, 116, 134, 135–36,
   139, 145; Winter, 33–35, 112, 141

Songs for Rain, 117
Sophia, Feast of, 119
Soul layers, 175–79, 185, 186, 207–8; in
   Autumn Equinox ritual, 207–8, 214
South Africa: Rain Queen Lovedu, 113,
   119. See also Swaziland Spain: and
   Angola, 191; Bull Running, 116;
   Santa Bárbara Africana, 203
Spirit: in creation, 19–20; family of,
   179–80; forgotten, 183; reborn,
   201. See also Ghosts
Spring, 73–111, 114–15, 200; deities,
   76–82; Equinox, 33, 98–99, 112,
   114; rituals, 81, 82–88, 95–96,
   97–111, 139–40
Spring Flowers, 114
Spring Maiden, 76–78, 86. See also Oshun
Starhawk, 9, 167
Stars, wishing, 150–55
Storytelling, 147. See also Tales
Summer, 116–17, 121–57; bride of, 117,
   139–41; deities, 122–25, 129,
   134–35, 138–39; New Orleans,
   142–45; rituals, 135, 136, 140–41,
   143–45, 147–55; Solstice, 33, 116,
   134, 135–36, 139, 145
Sun, 123–26, 133, 134, 135; associations
   with, 156–57; in Cancer, 134, 145,
   146; invocation to, 153; in Leo, 134,
   139, 145, 146; Midsummer placation
   of, 140–41; Mother of, 138–39; in
   Virgo, 145–46
Sun Goddess, 116, 123–24
Sunna, 124
Sunrise Dance, 117, 162
Sun Sister, 124
Swallows, depart Capistrano, 113, 119
Swastika, 194
Swaziland: King's Dance, 35, 112; She-
   Elephant Dance, 117
Sweden: Feast of St. Brigit, 117; Festival of
   Midsommar, 114, 136; Luciadagen,
   34, 119
Switzerland, Black Madonna, 117, 162
Symbols, planets associated with, 156

Tales, xiv–xv; authentic, xiv–xv, 26–27;
   composite, xv, 11–12; original, xv,
   11–12, 74, 88–90, 142–43

Taurus, 157
Thailand: Feast of River Goddess, 118; Festival of Floating Leaf Cups, 119; Ploughing Ceremony, 114
Thanksgiving, 2–4, 9, 118, 165, 201–2
Theresa, Miz, 4, 6–7
Three Mothers, Festival of, 118
Time, creation of, 19
Toba people, 124
Togo: Gelede, 198; Mamissi, 40–41; map, 16
Tonantzin, 116
Trinidad: Calinda dance, 144; Shango rituals, 204
Tuareg people, 162
Turtle Island, 141
Twins: Celebration of, 113, 119; Celestial, 125
Tyi Wara, 114

United Nations Day, 113, 119
Universal Soul, 175–76, 185, 207, 214
Unknowable One, 16
Uranus, associations with, 156–57

Valentine's Day, 113
Venus: associations with, 156–57; invocations to, 150–51
Vesta, Day of, 115
Virgen de Gaudalupe, 116, 119
Virginity, of Oshun, 80
Virgo, 157; Sun in, 145–46
Visitation of Our Lady, 137
Visualizations, guided, in rituals, 63–64
Voodoo: Africa's Secret Power (Chessi), 40–41
Voudou, 87, 143
Voudoun, 16–18, 143, 193

Washington, George, 201–2
Water: deities/Spirits, 39–43, 123–24; invocation to, 153; rituals, 39–43. *See also* Rain
West Africa, 16; Abiku, 118–19; Aje, 197–198; ancestor deification, 186–88; Gelede, 198; map, 16;

Mawu Day, 119; Sun, 133; Yam Festival, 116, 117, 163. *See also individual countries*
Wild Ones, 199
Winter, 21–72, 112–13, 200; deities, 25–26, 39–43, 48–51; rituals, 29–32, 39–43, 52–72, 112; Solstice, 33–35, 112, 141
Winter Nights, 118
Wisdom (Sophia), Feast of, 119
Wishing stars, 150–55
Witches: Aje, 197; season of, 164–68
Wodaabe people, 162
Women: gynophobia, 130; rituals celebrating, 9, 112, 115; Sexual Soul, 176. *See also* Matrilineal societies
Women and Girls, Celebration of, 112
Women's Fertility Day, 115
Workers, rituals celebrating, 91, 115
World Day for Animals, 118
World Environment Day, 114
World Food Day, 118

Yalode, 105
Yam Festival, 116, 117, 163–64
Yansa, 193
Yemaya, 39, 41–42; Feast of Yemaya and Oshun, 116, 162; rituals, 62–67, 116, 162
Yemonja, xi, xii, xvi, 24–29, 32; Elegba and, 49; names of, 32–33; poem for, 22–23
Yoruba people, xii; ancestor deification, 186, 189–90; creation myths, 12–13, 14, 15; deities, 16–17, 25, 49, 79, 124; *ebbo,* 72n; Gede, 155; on map, 16; proverbs, 170, 197; witches, 197–198; world beliefs, 170–72
Yucatan: Ix Chel, 78, 114. *See also* Maya

Zachary (Elizabeth's husband), 137
Zaire, Indombe, 124
Zimbabwe, Independence Day, 114
Zombies, 196
Zulu Parade, 84–88